FACING
SHERMAN
IN SOUTH CAROLINA

Facing Sherman in South Carolina

March Through the Swamps

SERIES EDITOR
DOUGLAS W. BOSTICK

CHRISTOPHER G. CRABB

Charleston   London

THE
History
PRESS

Published by The History Press
Charleston, SC 29403
www.historypress.net

Front cover: *War is Hell* by Mort Künstler.
© 2003 Mort Künstler, Inc. www.mkunstler.com

First published 2010

Manufactured in the United States

ISBN 978.1.60949.015.7

Library of Congress Cataloging-in-Publication Data

Crabb, Christopher G.
Facing Sherman in South Carolina : march through the swamps / Christopher G. Crabb.
p. cm.
Includes bibliographical references and index.
ISBN 978-1-60949-015-7
1. Sherman's March through the Carolinas. 2. Sherman's March through the Carolinas-
-Personal narratives. 3. Sherman, William T. (William Tecumseh), 1820-1891. 4. South
Carolina--History--Civil War, 1861-1865--Campaigns. 5. Swamps--South Carolina-
-History--19th century. 6. Rivers--South Carolina--History--19th century. 7. South
Carolina--History--Civil War, 1861-1865--Personal narratives. 8. United States--
History--Civil War, 1861-1865--Campaigns. 9. United States--History--Civil War,
1861-1865--Personal narratives. I. Title.
E477.7.C73 2010
975.7'03--dc22
2010043168

Contents

CONTENTS

Chapter 1

Will They Invade Us—Where Is Their Army?

That army of vengeance had arrived. It was men of the Left Wing of Major General William Tecumseh Sherman's 65,000-man gargantuan that had the distinction of being the first on South Carolina soil in an invasion many had hoped for the entire war. Ever since the perceived insult to the national colors that came with the firing on Fort Sumter, a collective mood of vengeance against the Palmetto State found its way into the minds of many men in blue. Longingly they dreamed of the day an army would march through South Carolina and punish that entity once remarked to be "too small to be a country, too large to be an insane asylum."

The redemption of a nation's sacred honor demanded such retribution in the minds of western boys from Illinois, Indiana, Wisconsin, Michigan, Ohio, Iowa and Minnesota. Eastern lads from Pennsylvania, New York, New Jersey, Connecticut and Massachusetts may have longingly dreamed of invading the state that in their minds instigated the fall of dominoes that led to the slaughter of their comrades at Chancellorsville, Gettysburg and Fredericksburg. In lockstep with these boys from north of the Mason-Dixon were men from border states Missouri and Kentucky, laying aside family and fraternity ties to follow "Uncle Billy."

Now the opportunity for this punitive invasion designed to cripple the Southern war effort had finally come. These veterans from all over the Union could now lock horns with the "sons of the chivalry," the best and the brightest of the state that aimed the first cannon in Charleston in the spring of 1861. But another enemy lay ahead, an enemy that couldn't be driven away with superior numbers: the South Carolina landscape. Rather than the sons of the Palmetto State, they would face a diversity of displaced Confederates holding endless myriad swamps, creeks and watercourses. It would take a special kind of army to cross through South Carolina, as this was no ordinary campaign. What kind of army that would be remained to be seen.

On December 30, 1864, Major General William Ward waited with his Third Division of the Twentieth Army Corps to cross the Savannah River into South Carolina. Born in Virginia, the Kentucky transplant perhaps would have taken a different path that did not include crossing the swollen Savannah had it not been for a childhood move by his parents.[1] As it has a way of doing, fate now placed Ward along the banks of the Savannah. Like in Charleston harbor four years before, a Kentuckian in blue stared across the water at South Carolina. Starting fresh the next morning, Ward's division crossed via a pontoon bridge to Hutchinson Island. The broad river made the island a spot of dry land dividing the river into two channels like a stone resting in the midst of a raging creek. Complications arose as the bridge was not yet complete. A soldier's companion through the ages—delay—marked the invasion's first moments.

Fortunately, three small boats made up the difference. Ironically, the largest invading army to ever step foot into South Carolina would first come ashore in small boatloads. Unfortunately, there was still more "hurry up and waiting" to do. It was the waiting that provided both misery and danger for Federals. Misery came with every ticking second as many of Ward's men had not been reoutfitted in Savannah, making the bone-chilling rain nearly unbearable. Danger also made its presence known. Protected by the swollen river, Rebel pickets added to the elements by raining down lead on the waiting Yankees. The fire was accurate enough to keep the hunkering Federals honest by killing a man of the 105th Illinois and wounding another of the 102nd Illinois.[2]

Elements of Colonel Henry Case's First Brigade were the first ashore in South Carolina. Driving off the pickets, the Yankees were now alone. Unfortunately, it would be unlikely that any comrades could be crossed over that night. Since a lodgment is only as safe as the reinforcements it can count on, Case's isolated spear point was withdrawn to Hutchinson Island. The delay was fitting. The crossing into South Carolina would open the new year. Throughout the following day, Case's entire brigade finally crossed the Savannah. Swatting away Rebel scouts, the vanguard pushed to a plantation five miles inland. It was here that their first taste of the reviled

Leading the way: Major General William T. Ward. *Courtesy of the Library of Congress.*

South Carolina chivalry would come. Not surprisingly, here the first taste of vengeance against the state would manifest itself.

Predictably, it was quite a cold night for the newly arrived Yankees. According to Stephen Fleharty of the 102nd Illinois, it did not take too much imagination to make their stay more comfortable. After all, they "were in South Carolina," a state that hardly endeared itself to Sherman's vengeful command. One Union soldier described this callous feeling with his hope that the state "should be pretty thoroughly overhauled" and that rebellion should soon "play out all around." Before long, unoccupied houses and barns were torn down as replacement firewood for nearby wet green pine. Only the owner's home, a "very large, elaborately furnished, two story gothic mansion," and an overseer's home temporarily escaped destruction as Union officers conscripted them into service.

Remorse was rare, as the plantation belonged to Dr. Langdon Cheves, a prominent South Carolina secessionist. Cheves certainly had a material stake in the antebellum issues of slavery and states' rights. In "happier" days, Cheves's plantation had prospered to the tune of $700,000 annually, according to one of his new Yankee squatters. Of more consequence was another discovery. A prewar speech found among his papers encouraged at least one soldier's snickers. In a speech fifteen years before, Cheves responded to warnings of a Northern military response to secession with the jingoistic retort, "Will they invade us—where is their army??" The phantom Yankee army had arrived and was ransacking his plantation. Ironically, it was now his Confederate countrymen who were nowhere to be found. It was an irony that could not have escaped Yankees marauding across his property.[3]

Case's advance inland sent a lightning bolt through the Confederate command. His brigade's rapid progress forced Lieutenant General Joseph Wheeler's cavalry to watch a very real threat. Wheeler's cavalrymen hugged Case's columns gathering intelligence. Unsurprisingly, information was sketchy. Only reports of half-mile-long Federal columns and arriving steamboats offered any clues.[4] Neither report was promising for Confederates screening the Yankee advance.

Likely the inspiration of the alarming reports, the balance of Ward's division had crossed into South Carolina at Screven's Ferry. By January 2, most had taken the more expedient method of travel by the steamer *Planter*. The *Planter*'s involvement is notable to say the least. Incidentally, the vessel was in Federal hands after its African American pilot, Robert Smalls, brought it into Union lines. Thus, poetic justice was afoot as the steamer clipped toward the shore.

Two days later, Case's men slung on knapsacks and blanket rolls. Behind a line of skirmishers, the column moved again. Facing only a few scouts, Case's brigade easily seized the abandoned Confederate fortifications at Hardee Plantation a mile away. Situated on commanding ground, "Fort Hardee's" three-acre site boasted a strong earthwork that could protect over two thousand men. Bolstering things, embrasures provided protection for enough artillery to stock an army.[5] If fully manned, the garrison could hold off an enemy multiple times its number. Ward's men wiped their brows in relief that a couple thousand Confederates elected not to remain in the grass-covered fort.

As at Cheves Plantation, the new location was quickly dismantled board by board. The standard "gloves off" mood still prevailed. As one Yankee candidly recalled, "We were under the same kind of orders as in Georgia but the feelings of resentment against South Carolina were different than those against Georgia."[6] One Yankee recalled the resulting "perfect bedlam":

> *At that place another dash was made on the vacant buildings. The men had scarcely broken ranks, when the click of a solitary hammer was heard; it was quickly followed by others, and soon dozens were at work, creating a perfect bedlam,—hack, bang, rip, rattle, squeak, crash,—and the boards flew and the beams fell faster than they were ever made to fly or fall by any Hook and Ladder company. Men were all over and all through the houses, perfectly reckless of flying boards and falling timbers. At length they commenced cutting the corner posts of one of the buildings. Soon it began to totter. The men were on tip-toe. A few more strokes of the axe were sufficient, and down came the structure, raising a cloud of dust. There was a yell, a blind rush, and a scramble. A few moments sufficed to remove the last stick of timber, leaving the ground ready for the plow.[7]*

Simultaneously, the rest of the division arrived. As before, the Rebel forces offered little opposition. Fallen trees, distant campfires and the absence or carcass of every sustenance-giving beast were the only signs that the Rebels even existed nearby. Despite the Confederates' best efforts, sustenance remained providing there was the right share of resentment. A man of the Eighty-fifth Indiana, whose pious commitment to reading his testament did not prevent such resentment, offers a humorous anecdote of just that.

According to a comrade, this devout Yankee left on his foraging rounds chided to "read his testament diligently and say his prayers very devoutly" for the hunger of his comrades required his "best stealing." The soldier flourished in his crusade at Hardee Plantation. When the Bible-toting forager arrived with a mule loaded with ham, chickens and sweet potatoes, he whipped out a rather large, embroidered feather bolster. To his comrades' amusement, the fellow sneered, "These Rebels kicked up this Rebellion and I have come down to help put it down, and I'm going to have a soft place to lay my old head on one night, yes I am!"[8]

In a finale to the nightmare occurring at the "high toned chivalry" of Dr. Cheves's plantation, some Union troops remained behind, throwing up a camp with the boards and bricks of slave shanties among the orange, palmetto and live oak trees. These four-foot-high shelters served as a "beautiful camp," and life was easy. As usual, officers had "tolerably, festive times" in the plantation homes. Eventually, the idyllic life would end as the men rejoined the division, leaving Cheves's and his son's mansions "to ashes."[9]

Confederates did echo a painfully prophetic cry as they retreated before the Yankee column. For those "having ears to hear," the admonishment "The Yankees are coming" rang out.[10] The insertion by one brigade had grown to a full Federal division on South Carolina soil.

Chapter 2

You'd Better Get Out; We Are the Fifteenth Corps

Fear is a pervasive entity, gobbling up everything in its path. Throughout the war, South Carolinians watched their coast, dreading a sea-borne Federal invasion. That moment had finally arrived, and it truly seemed time to get out of the way. With the Left Wing establishing a firm foothold, the Right Wing under Major General Oliver Howard set out in motion. On January 3, 1865, the Seventeenth Corps began embarking on transports at Fort Thunderbolt near Savannah, Georgia. Their objective was a move to the South Carolina coast at Beaufort. By January 11, the Seventeenth Corps had completed their journey. Their Right Wing counterparts, the Fifteenth Corps, would follow in their wake.

On January 13, 1865, the Seventeenth Corps moved from Beaufort toward the Charleston–Savannah Railroad at Pocotaligo on the South Carolina mainland. The corps, under Major General Francis Preston Blair, would first have to cross the deceptively named Whale Branch. A key figurehead in the Unionist cause in Missouri, Blair could relate to the beleaguered citizens of South Carolina in at least one respect. Like his most esteemed opponents of the Carolina chivalry, Blair was seemingly a part of the hypocritical system of slavery that he spent his prewar years attempting to contain as a "Free Soil" congressman. Though instrumental in helping to save Missouri for the Union, Blair would fail to endear himself to radical Republicans stemming from his desire to offer gracious terms to the defeated South.[11] Any kindred backgrounds broke down when the slaveholding Blair entered the state that gave birth to the movement that ripped the now eighty-five-year-old Union in two.

Sherman's not-so-secret weapon, the pontoon bridge. *Courtesy of the Library of Congress.*

Getting things off to a start, a party under Lieutenant Colonel D.T. Kirby of Blair's staff crossed Whale Branch via a boat and covered the construction of a pontoon bridge. The pontoon's simple layout helped in the task. The floating pontoons would simply be strung across the water by tying off to the opposite bank and then covered with planks. This particular occasion required a six-hundred-foot span of bridging. By the next morning, the Federals had constructed the floating thoroughfare and were ready for crossing.

The Third Division led the corps across. Whatever Confederates were still around would choose another location to show any pluck. That place was five miles from the ferry. It was here where one of the first signs of resistance reared its head. At Horspa Bridge near Gardens Corner waited the Third South Carolina Cavalry and a detachment of other commands, all under Colonel C.J. Colcock. Looking to temporarily check the Yankees, Colcock's men manned a strong set of earthworks supported by a few artillery pieces. Strengthening the position against a frontal assault was a boggy, four-hundred-yard-wide salt marsh. Despite such advantages, Colcock's options were limited. Though he blocked one road from the ferry, another by way of Sheldon Church posed an easy route around his flank. To cover that approach, Colcock could post only a couple of companies. The remainder of his 150 troopers waited along Horspa Creek.[12]

The ground Colcock chose to defend was hardly virgin territory, as frequent Federal incursions to seize Pocotaligo passed through the area. This made these roads old witnesses to outnumbered Rebels attempting to parry Yankee thrusts. These earlier attempts were turned back by a combination of Confederate pluck and sluggish Federal movements. At the very least, these old skirmishes had to give Colcock a glimmer of hope of slowing down this new Yankee column.

Around 10:00 a.m., Blair's men struck Colcock's thin defenses along the creek. The Federals conjured up just enough musketry and shelling to keep the Rebels occupied. Meanwhile, a Yankee brigade moved via the feebly guarded Sheldon Church Road. The long-distance skirmishing continued until around 3:00 p.m. when Colcock realized he had been outflanked. On the Sheldon Church Road, his meek detachment tumbled backward, unable to stem the blue tide. One prominent casualty would be the road's namesake, Sheldon Church. Like the British almost a century before, Sherman's men burned the beautiful Greek Revival structure.

One anecdote highlights how dangerous even an outnumbered enemy can be. As Right Wing commander O.O. Howard scouted the Confederate line, a Rebel sharpshooter drew a bead. Three or four shots struck uncomfortably close before Howard and his aide dashed to safety behind their own skirmishers. Howard did offer up a "polite bow" for the Southerner's "charming salute" before bailing.[13] Even assuming that Howard's martial glory was less dramatic than he recollected, it still evidenced that the Confederates were dangerous. Howard's incident was a nice reminder that he would need to give Confederates a wider berth when reconnoitering. It was a lesson he would soon nearly pay with his life for failing to learn.

His flank turned, Colcock retreated to Stony Creek. If he expected any better fortunes, he would be sadly mistaken. The Federals had outguessed him and moved a brigade via a parallel road to turn the position. In a sign of things to come, for the second straight time strong Confederate earthworks were emptied as Colcock retreated. Colcock's failure to make a fight at Stony Creek still produced at least one casualty. The nearby Stony Creek Presbyterian Church was torn down for Yankee bridging material.

Leaving a screen of skirmishers, Colcock's men retired into the entrenchments at Pocotaligo to await the Yankees once more. Bolstering the

A survivor throughout: Major General O.O. Howard, Right Wing commander. *Courtesy of the Library of Congress.*

arriving troopers was the division of Major General Lafayette McLaws. A native of Augusta, Georgia, McLaws was a West Pointer whose solid service in Virginia made him more than capable to handle the task at hand. The main blight on his otherwise solid career was a charge by former classmate and superior James Longstreet over preparations in the failed assault of Fort Sanders near Knoxville, Tennessee. Although vindicated by President Davis, the controversy nevertheless led to McLaws's trip south.[14]

Regardless of semantics, the Rebel forces manning the works could certainly use the experienced former subordinate of Robert E. Lee. Perhaps forgotten considering the circumstances, McLaws would likely spend his birthday of January 15 within earshot of fifteen thousand Yankees. With two thousand well-led troops entrenched at Pocotaligo, it would seem that finally the Confederates would slow Sherman's uncontested advance.

This Confederate passivity was not lost on contemporary observers. Lieutenant General William Hardee, commanding Confederate forces in Charleston, South Carolina, in particular lamented Colcock's timidity to Lieutenant General Wheeler. "Take charge of Colcock's cavalry and see that it fights. I fear that it did not win any laurels yesterday," was his pejorative observation.[15] Colcock's hard-pressed troopers would probably contend that a couple hundred men could only do so much.

Just as the sun began retreating beneath the horizon, Federal troops appeared at Pocotaligo. Like before, the Confederates had chosen their position well. Thick swamp covered their front. To see just what the earthworks concealed, Federal skirmishers probed forward. Bumping into their counterparts, the Yankees had driven in the Rebel outliers by nightfall.

Perhaps it was Colcock's hasty retreat, or maybe the Right Wing chief suffered from an understandable case of paternalistic pride. Either way, the fire from the fort didn't worry Howard too terribly. McLaws's men appeared "panicky," firing rapidly with little aim. Outside the fort, Yankees even tried psychological warfare by bellowing, "You'd better get out; we are the Fifteenth Corps!" Whatever poise the Confederate riflemen lacked in Howard's eyes, the Rebel artillery had his total respect. Mixed with Yankee counterparts, it gave a "noise like thunder" throughout the night as it echoed through the dark swamp.[16]

Along with the "spasmodic" musketry, the skirmishers developed at least five artillery pieces as they approached the fort from three sides. With darkness approaching, the Federals needed to go no farther. Far less costly than frontal assaults, the day's fighting had left around ten Federal casualties.[17] Apparently some of the Rebels were not quite as panicky as Howard remembered them.

The character of the ground and earthworks had to play on the minds of the Federal soldiers that night. A simple, solid battle plan would be needed to dislodge the Confederates with minimal loss of life. The next morning, Blair would leave a division entrenched before the fort, while slipping his two remaining divisions to turn the Confederate position. Like before, the best way to pass a fortified swamp crossing was around it.

As morning broke, devoutly religious Howard probably lamented having to fight on a Sunday. Like his adversary, Howard's path had its share of controversy. Howard's Eleventh Corps was roughed up badly in the early moments of Stonewall Jackson's flank attack at Chancellorville, Virginia.[18] The very fact that Howard now commanded the Right Wing was arguably surprising in itself. Howard, whose past had hardly been spectacular, could certainly not afford a swamp full of dead marking another rough handling. That dilemma would have been an absolute nightmare scenario. Fortunately for Howard, both his reputation and the sanctity of the Lord's day were safe, as the Confederates "got out" after all. Perhaps surmising that the Yankees had shown little intention of a direct assault so far, McLaws withdrew his men from the fort during the night. Fortunately for McLaws, his birthday would not be marked with the brutal business of war.

With a grand total of a dozen casualties, the Federals had driven ten miles and seized an important point on the Charleston–Savannah Railroad. The relative ease of the march to Pocotaligo was not lost on their chieftain. Sherman would later express surprise with how easily Pocotaligo was captured. In an admission that illustrated much of the anti-Carolina rhetoric within the army, Sherman noted that "taunting messages had also come to us, when in Georgia, to the effect that, when we should reach South Carolina, we should find a people less passive, who would fight us to the bitter end, daring us to come over, etc…I had every reason to expect bold and strong resistance at the many broad and deep rivers that lay across our path."[19] Considering such buildup, Sherman's surprise at South Carolina's apparent passivity is explicable. Much more was expected from the South Carolina chivalry.

Here at newly won Pocotaligo, Howard awaited the arrival of the other half of his wing, the Fifteenth Corps.[20] With its entire First Division and most of the Second Division either en route to or at Beaufort, the remaining Third and Fourth Divisions would move overland from Savannah to Pocotaligo. Early January 19, Major General John Smith's Third Division crossed into South Carolina. Smith did perhaps no greater service to his nation than a mere recommendation. Early in the war, the former jeweler from Galena, Illinois, helped discover a diamond in the rough when he recommended an obscure former army officer named U.S. Grant to his state's governor as a good man to raise a regiment.[21]

Oddly, his division had only two brigades. Thus, when Smith led Colonel C.R. Wever's Second Brigade across the pontoon to Hutchinson's and Pennyworth Islands, he would have one less command to cross. Unfortunately for Smith, Wever's arrival found only a narrow causeway reaching the area's main north–south artery, the Union Causeway. Consequently, wagons crossing the thin thoroughfare had little margin of error. The situation went bad quickly as a light rain began to fall around 9:30 a.m. Stepping up his movements to the Union Causeway and the New River Bridge, Smith hastened Wever's brigade forward to clear the road. By 2:00 p.m., Wever and most of the division wagon train halted near New Bridge after a twelve-mile march. All was good so far.

The good fortune was not found in the rear. Around 11:00 p.m., the skies opened up into a furious frenzy. Heavy rainfall swelled the surrounding lowlands, ripping away low points along the causeway. The ruined roads halted wagons directly in front of the next brigade in line—Colonel J.B. McCown's First Brigade—cutting off its advance. One unfortunate staff officer tried in vain to find a way to expedite McCown's men through the muck. He soon found himself wading through water up to his armpits. For three miles along the river, the land lay submerged. A new enemy had been found in the South Carolina lowlands. It was an enemy that was here to stay.

The following morning, Smith got a first glimpse of the watery wasteland. Admitting defeat to the elements, Smith ordered McCown back to Savannah to embark his brigade. Nine wagons, unable to be extracted, were abandoned as silent reminders of Mother Nature's wrath. Another reminder awaited discovery shortly. Arriving back near New Bridge, Smith found only a meager meal of pig's feet and hardtack waiting. Upon inquiry, Smith learned the fare was about as well as could be expected when eating without mess gear. And Mother Nature's fury was directly responsible.

It was a story that would ordinarily be humorous. By nightfall, a shell of water six inches to two feet deep lay across Smith's camp. Though hard to tell, their encampment was once part of one of the area's many plantations. As men walked, occasionally they would suddenly disappear, much to the "merriment" of comrades. It seems the plantation was riddled with twelve- to fifteen-foot wells that were now submerged. In one of the "merry" incidents, Smith's messmate was one of the unlucky lads to suddenly disappear, leaving the mess gear down somewhere in the submerged cavity. Smith could thank the flooded landscape for his Spartan fare.

Difficulties aside, Smith managed to get Wever across New River the next day. The problems continued as a rainy eleven-mile march ended three miles short of Hazzard's Bridge. Along the way, three miles of the road lay submerged under one to two feet of water. It took building seven small bridges and 380 yards of corduroying to keep the column moving. The following day, Smith marched another twelve miles, crossed Hazzard's Bridge and encamped near Bee's Creek in another day of hard rainfall. Four miles of his march was over a submerged road through swamps, requiring the building of seventy feet of bridges. On January 23, the task finally paid off as the ten-mile march ended near Pocotaligo after another rainy day with another 480 yards of road corduroyed. But Smith had found his way to his comrades.[22] And not a single Rebel had delayed his column. It must have seemed to many Yankee hearts that Mother Nature was wearing gray.

Smith had corduroyed his way through to Pocotaligo, but it was clear there was no following in his footsteps. McCown's boat ride would end at Beaufort and inevitably Pocotaligo. Major General John M. Corse's Fourth Division would take a different tack. Blocked by the morass along the river, Corse would march his Fourth Division with the Fourteenth Corps to cross at Sister's Ferry. It would be later at another overflowed river that Corse's command would rejoin their Fifteenth Corps comrades.

Chapter 3

There Goes Your Old Gospel Shop

Often in times of war, few things are held sacred. As Yankees flooded into South Carolina, few indications were offered that they would break this timeless maxim. With two firm footholds, Sherman's army had achieved a fine start. With vengeance in their hearts, everything under the sun was fair game for Sherman's men. As the breach widened, more and more opportunity would come to utterly devastate all in their way. It was frightening news for the unfortunate souls caught in their path.

Early success notwithstanding, Sherman's troops were forced into a waiting game. At best, Sherman had only a little more than a large corps on South Carolina soil. The balance of his over sixty thousand men was either at sea or moving with the Fourteenth Corps to Sister's Ferry. Meanwhile, Confederate officers shuttled troops to meet potential threats. These threats began to materialize as the Twentieth Corps began to nibble more at the feeble Confederate psyche. Following in Ward's wake, Brigadier General Nathaniel Jackson's First Division crossed the Savannah on January 17. As a former machinist from Massachusetts, Jackson could certainly appreciate the tough labor required to get his division across the Savannah.[23]

The crossing of the swollen river was far from tranquil. Sergeant Rice C. Bull of the 123rd New York recalled vividly the swaying pontoon bridges that shook with each tramp of feet.[24] "Rocking" trip that it was, Bull and his comrades reached South Carolina safely. The division marched seven miles beyond the river, striking their bivouac at Ward's old campground, the devastated Cheves Plantation.

Once again, the plantation saw invaders fill its grounds. The consolidation of the entire Twentieth Corps in South Carolina was cut short via the Savannah overflowing its banks, submerging much of the corduroyed roads. The resulting surge prevented Brigadier General John Geary's Second Division from crossing. Like Corse's Fifteenth Corps division, Geary's men would have to join the Fourteenth Corps in crossing at Sister's Ferry. Consequently, both the Fifteenth and Twentieth Corps would begin the campaign "short" a division.[25]

While Jackson crossed, Ward left his camp on Hardee Plantation. Constant drilling, scouting and general camp life had filled the past eleven days. His destination was the nondescript town of Hardeeville, South Carolina. Its only real value lay in its status as a station on the Charleston–Savannah Railroad. Overawed by the sudden surge in Yankee visitors, Confederates were nowhere to be found. Ward reached Hardeeville uneventfully, delayed only by fallen timber. The Rebel "lumberjacks" had wisely taken little interest to stand in the way.

As was a fixture thus far, the elements made up for defunct Rebel resistance. A week's worth of rainfall made the roads "deep under mud and water" while mules and wagons disappeared out of sight. In the words of a Union soldier, the whole country around stranded Hardeeville was now "afloat."[26] Clearly, running supplies the way they came in would be a difficult proposition.

With the rain-induced freshet in mind, Ward halted two of his brigades at Hardeeville and sent Brigadier General Daniel Dustin's Second Brigade a few miles to the old steamboat landing at Purysburg. The town, despite its history dating back to the American Revolution's Savannah Campaign, was now deserted ruins.[27] Located conveniently on the Savannah, the dead settlement did offer a link to the Federal supply boats. With their old route now under water, Purysburg was the new Yankee "cracker" line. Dustin's men settled in unloading supplies and scouting the surrounding countryside for Confederates.[28]

Dustin's men received company, as Jackson soon moved from Cheves Plantation to Purysburg. Misery reigned on January 18, as it took fortuitously located pine knots to keep Jackson's encamped men warm that night. The comforting glow of campfires was squelched, however, as the sky opened up around midnight, pelting Jackson's hard-luck command throughout the following day. Nearby, Smith's men could relate as they sloshed through rain-swollen fields and disappeared into submerged wells.

The trip had been a crash lesson in the hard hand of war. Burned homes littered the countryside as visible reminders of the Federal presence. Making matters worse, Jackson's route carried the soaked Federals through the remains of Hardeeville. In the words of recently drenched Rice C. Bull, "not much was left standing." Ward's division had utterly wrecked the town. The town's shocking appearance led at least one Federal to describe it as "war struck."[29] Scarcely a better description can be expected for the first town overrun in the "cradle of secession." Fortunately, for one with the delicate sensibilities of a chaplain, Hardeeville's destruction at least bore some resemblance to military necessity:

> In less than half hour all those buildings were tore down and piled in Rowes Ready to convert into Camps for Each Company. This being done then we took the shingles and slivered planks and frames made fires and in no time were sipping away at our hot coffee mixing up a little with hard tack and sowbelly as composed as tho Hardeeville was still standing and in her great glory. I was making some remarks on this scene. "Hump," says the boys, "this is nothing. The place is so small we had not sea Room sufficient. If you had been with us on our big march you would have seen sights then." Well you see having just came into the sheepfold I am green, yet but I'll soon get used to it no doubt.[30]

Another Union soldier recounted the town's deserted homes torn down in a hurry, and the ever-important "fairly waterproof" camp shanties went up quickly.[31] In the words of one Yankee, these huts were for mere comfort as the cold, rainy weather and piercing winds made for a disagreeable stay during the occupation. With almost ankle-deep water and mud deluging the camps, men took to robbing brush from nearby pines to line the bottom of their tents.[32] Thus, what was once a small Southern town had now become a glorified encampment with its buildings providing necessary lumber. War truly was hell, and few things under heaven could stand up to its fury. Probably much to the chagrin of our pious eyewitness of Hardeeville's chastisement, even a church was not spared the Yankee wrath. During the destruction, another correspondent painted a picture that was hardly pretty and most assuredly not Christian:

> Again the work of destroying buildings commenced, Among others, a large beautiful church was attacked. Men of various regiments were engaged in the work. First the pulpit and seats were torn out, then the siding and the blinds were ripped off. Many axes were at work. The corner posts were cut, the building tottered, the beautiful spire, up among the green trees, leaned for

"There goes your d——d old gospel shop": the ruins of Sheldon Church. *Courtesy of the author.*

a time several degrees out of the perpendicular, vibrating to and fro. A tree that stood in the way was cut. By the use of long poles the men increased the vibratory motion of the building, and soon, with a screeching groan the spire sunk down amidst the timbers which gave way beneath, and as the structure became a pile of rubbish, some of the most wicked of the raiders yelled out: "There goes your d——d old gospel shop."

Scarcely a vestige of the "old gospel shop" was visible the following day. Ambivalently, the Yankee witness proclaimed the "barbarous" assault as fulfillment of the words of scripture, "For they have sown the wind and they shall reap the whirlwind."[33] At least some destruction was legitimate, as the nearby Charleston–Savannah Railroad was wrecked. Between providing shelter from the terrible elements and having a militarily important railroad wrecked, the town's destruction had both military and punitive value. Unfortunately, Hardeeville would not be the last town virtually obliterated by Sherman's army. In all, over half a dozen towns would be totally or almost destroyed by Sherman's troops on the march to Columbia. It is a chilling prospect to think of how destructive an army can be. For South Carolinians in early 1865, this prospect was a reality.

Jackson's troops reached Purysburg by January 20 and awaited the next grand move. Their idle position allowed them to watch with disgust the rainfall that would mar the coming days. The roads became muddy quagmires before their very eyes while men hoped against hope that they would dry before the march resumed. Unfortunately for the new arrivals, the rainfall raised water levels, flooding the Yankee camps.[34]

It would be difficult to overstate the flooding that marred the countryside. A later recollection from the Second Massachusetts described the bone-chilling, miserable weather: "The weather was stormy and the water high, flooding the roads and all the country for miles, and one storm only seemed to give place to another." The roads and country were not alone in the flooding. In flooding of deluge proportions, a Federal chaplain recalled the waters literally transforming the camp into an island, with the flooded roads restricting movement beyond. In one humorous example, one ill-fated Union officer laid down in his tent for the night only to wake up surrounded by water. Men of the Third Wisconsin found the unsettling dilemma of finding their company streets filled with knee-deep water.

Even mundane duties became feats of incredible difficulty. Pickets stood post in canoes and scows as nearby swamps had expanded into "lakes of shiny mud."[35] Experiences like that at Purysburg bore no small role in our aforementioned minister's desire that countrymen impatient with the army's progress be forced to wade through the South Carolina swamps during the high water times.[36] Such retribution should certainly illustrate to them, as it does to us, the experiences so far in the campaign.

With the arrival of McCown's brigade in South Carolina on January 26, the Right Wing was now concentrated, and the majority of the Twentieth Corps was now near Hardeeville. The time had come for Sherman's army to begin their advance inland. All was not perfect, and there was one major snag. High waters still had the entire Fourteenth Corps, cavalry and two other divisions stranded across the Savannah. As it looked, Sherman's entire force would not begin the campaign together. In particular, Sherman feared this delay, forcing his army to use valuable resources, while allowing Lieutenant General John Bell Hood's Army of Tennessee to affect a junction with troops already in South Carolina.[37] Despite such concerns—and because of them—the march must continue.

Chapter 4

They Are South Carolinians, Not Americans

Civic pride was hardly a trait unique to nineteenth-century South Carolinians. Regardless, the Twentieth Corps was about to tramp through one of the wealthiest areas of the state where "King Cotton" and all that it entailed were as prominent as the sun. Opulent plantations and their grandeur were on display as the columns marched. For these longtime veterans of some of the Army of the Potomac's most bloody battles, the wealth on display was probably a bitter reminder of the class of South Carolinians whom they perceived had unilaterally brought war on the nation. Their chance had come to punish those who, in their minds, valued loyalty to state over the Union.

On January 26, Jackson moved to secure Sister's Ferry, the Savannah River crossing for the balance of the Left Wing. The crossing was now more important than ever for a more practical reason for Twentieth Corps commander Major General Alpheus S. Williams. The heavy rainfall and the resulting flooding had crippled the overland supply routes. Although Purysburg had worked as a stopgap, the roads branching from it were now prone to going from passable to horrendous in a short time. The sooner reinforcements in man and material were available upstream at Sister's Ferry, the more stable the situation would become.

Jackson dispatched Brigadier General William Hawley's Second Brigade up the Sister's Ferry Road in search of its namesake. The past week of heavy rainfall unleashed its vengeance as Yankees plodded along. Submerged fallen trees lined the road, forcing Hawley's men to clear the frequent interruptions.

Others sank up to their knees in the mud lining the road and swamps.[38] Chagrined, Hawley's command moved only nine miles in two days before halting at a plantation nine miles from Robertville. By January 28, Jackson's entire division had passed the quagmire. It was hardly a pleasant trip.

The lodgment placed Jackson's division at a crossroads of the Sister's Ferry Road with that from Robertville. Their objective ahead, Jackson pushed Colonel James Selfridge's First Brigade toward the ferry. Down the road lay the crossing that would, by necessity, have to replace Purysburg as the new supply link. Selfridge dispatched five companies of the 123rd New York under Major Tanner forward to examine what lay ahead. Two miles into his foray, Tanner's discovery was far from comforting.

The New Yorkers found swollen Cypress Creek and its adjoining swamp across their path. Unfortunately, the creek's bridge had been a victim of the rising water table and had been washed away. Complicating matters, the causeway through the swamp was now submerged under the familiar knee-deep water. Gamely, Selfridge's entire brigade was moved down to try and corduroy their way through. Despite the old "college try," the Federals soon gave up. Once again, Mother Nature had done what phantom Confederates failed to do—turned back a Yankee column.

Rather than plod through the impassable mire, Williams backtracked and marched toward Robertville. The town was already expected to be a destination for the Left Wing. The only alteration would be that Sister's Ferry would be reached faster from Robertville over presumably much better roads and with less effort. Despite the modification, Williams's waterlogged corps was still not out of the "water." Ward's division at Hardeeville still had to rejoin Jackson's division.

With the reports of rising waters via local civilians, Williams intended to get Ward's division on the clear road to Robertville as soon as possible. The rising waters, along with the prospect of several days before Sister's Ferry would be operational, meant that the quicker Ward reached Jackson, the better. The adventures of Smith's divided division on January 19–20 certainly made such problems all too real. Failure to act promptly could cripple the Twentieth Corps in a larger-scale version of Smith's earlier troubles.

Reunited, Jackson's division led the corps as it made a beeline for Robertville early on January 29. As usual, fallen trees barred the road. Countering the desperate ploy, the 143rd New York went to work clearing the annoying obstructions. Mud and water covered the roads, forcing Yankees to constantly search the country for fence rails and poles to corduroy the roads for passage.[39] For the undermanned Confederates, fallen trees served as a bloodless impediment to slow the endless columns of Federals.

Not all obstructions were inanimate. Small parties of Rebel cavalry hovered on the column's flanks to pick up a scent or possibly snatch up a few straying Yankees. The march was moving along uneventfully, when around 11:00 a.m. the sounds of gunfire reverberated ahead. The New Yorkers put down the axe and took up the rifle to enter the fray. The Yankees shoved a party of Confederate horsemen back to within a mile of the town before Hawley's brigade arrived on the scene in relief.[40]

Reigning in, a few hundred Rebel troopers waited outside Robertville. Hawley shook out a couple of companies of the Third Wisconsin to drive the Confederates across Black Swamp Creek. The Confederate troopers obliged the Yankees in a short duel before giving way. With Federals in pursuit, the horsemen fell back to and through the town. As the Southerners clopped away, a final heavy volley hastened their withdrawal.[41] Their rapid retreat had left behind one man to capture; however, their fire had wounded three Federals.[42] With only a little mischief, Jackson's division had captured Robertville. Originally settled before the American Revolution, the hamlet once bore the name of Black Swamp in honor of the nearby bog draining the area. Ironically, the town was once a part of the now defunct "Lincoln County." The army of a very different Lincoln had now arrived.

The town itself was a jewel of the region, serving as the hub of an area of enormous wealth from the varying plantations. Robertville was a fine example of the wealth generated in nineteenth-century South Carolina through cotton and all that it implied. By the beginning of the war, Robertville was the closest settlement for a number of plantations that would make any nineteenth-century planter proud. Plantations administered by as many as fifty to two hundred slaves were a norm while some had as many as five hundred slaves working the crops. In a telling statistic, one study found at least 440 South Carolinians were considered "millionaires" (which meant that they held more than one hundred slaves). St. Peter's Parish, of which Robertville belonged, itself had 19. Naturally, some of the homes of these great planters reflected such wealth and privilege. If the Twentieth Corps was looking for an area with some of South Carolina's gentry to punish, they had found it.

Robertville offered the conveniences needed by such affluence. A schoolteacher, perhaps an example of the hamlet's prosperity, described the town in such pleasant terms: "A splendid village with six houses, a church, and academy, two stores and a blacksmith shop. But there are a number of houses situated at unequal distances around it, and inhabited by wealthy planters." Though many were absentees with less luxurious homes around town reflecting this fact, sizeable holdings and wealth flowed from Robertville and its surrounding plantations. A notable institution was the Black Swamp Baptist Church that met the town's spiritual needs. The building reflected its parishioners as its cypress exterior was blessed with three coats of "the best English lead white paint." Equally notable was the Robertville Academy, as education in polite society was of particular importance.[43]

The product of such a blend of education and refinement provides a glimpse of the destruction that beset Robertville. Mrs. Nancy Bostick DeSaussure was picking oranges at her family's home when slaves came running in a "state of wild excitement" proclaiming that Yankees were nearby. DeSaussure, whose home and grounds had only weeks before hosted Wheeler's retreating cavalry, fled like many of her neighbors. Trying to protect her home, DeSaussure left on her mantel images struck of former schoolmates from her time in a Northern finishing school. Her hope was that one of Sherman's raiders would recognize one of the faces and preserve the home from destruction.[44]

One young soldier found an image of his sister amid the mementos and, moved with emotion, wrote DeSaussure after the war of seeing "amidst the roar of battle the likeness of his angel sister." His beloved sibling had perished by the time Yankees swarmed the DeSaussure home. Unfortunately for DeSaussure, the soldier's comrades were hardly moved by such displays and burned her home to the ground.

As the charred remnants of her home attest, DeSaussure would have been better off pleading her case in person. As Sherman's men crossed the Savannah River, one soldier captured the mood of an army by exhorting comrades, "Boys, this is old South Carolina, let's give her hell."[45] Hell is exactly what they had in mind for Robertville. Another witness also noted the abandoned homesteads in their path. Writing to his sister, his words are stunning in their candor:

> *All wealthy people have fled their approach, leaving splendid plantations and palatial mansions and refugee farther into the state only to be troubled soon again to pack up their trunk and flee still farther as the yanks advance. The poor people are respected by the soldiers and their property protected, while the rich are persecuted when caught and barns, gins, and houses fall victim to the invader's match.*[46]

The particular disgust with the region's wealthy disclosed a trend that seemed to permeate significant portions of Sherman's army. South Carolina bore the distinction of firing the first shots on Fort Sumter. Coupled with the state's much-lauded role as the first state to secede from the Union, the Palmetto State was seen by many in Sherman's army as the source of the tragedy that was the Civil War. "South Carolina, the cradle of secession, must suffer," seemed to be a refrain on the minds of many of Sherman's troops.

A South Carolinian along Sherman's path in Georgia noticed a marked change in Yankee sentiments when it came to the fate of the Palmetto State. "The Yanks had threatened South Carolina, saying they would not leave a house standing. After they found out I was from this state, they would say all they could in my presence to aggravate."[47] Truly, the men of Sherman's army had it in for South Carolina and were prepared to lay waste to the state for its "sins."

Most despised among South Carolinians was the chivalry. Loosely defined, the chivalry was the state's perceived gentlemen class that had precipitated the war, fought as its most proud warriors and believed so strongly in its battlefield success. In mocking derision, one Union officer saw Confederate passivity in South Carolina as a repudiation of the noble pretensions he perceived from South Carolinians. Describing the South Carolina chivalry, he chided that "these fellows who were to die in the last ditch, who would welcome us with bloody hands to hospitable graves, are more cowardly than children, and whine like whipped schoolboys."[48]

Another man of the Seventy-third Ohio chronicled with amusement the "bold, defiant, last ditch, fire-eating South Carolinians" being as "harmless as babes" as Yankees invaded their state.[49] While in South Carolina, Sherman's men doubtlessly expected to soon lock horns with the sons of South Carolina's leading secessionists who had allegedly swore so vehemently to defend their state and luxurious firesides. One officer likely had the chivalry in mind when he commented, "The higher classes represent the scum, and the lower the dregs of civilization. They are South Carolinians, not Americans."[50]

Even the higher calling of gospel minister didn't always block this disposition. The chaplain of the Seventy-eighth Ohio found little to revere the "sacred soil" of South Carolina when he made sport of the "land of in invincible chivalry" being subdued so easily by Sherman's army.[51] As the men of the Twentieth Corps looked around Robertville, there were no doubt thoughts like these running through at least some of their minds at the sight of many homes of South Carolina planters standing there abandoned, with the state's sons nowhere to be found.

The destruction of Ingleside—the home of B.R. Bostick, father of the beleaguered Mrs. DeSaussure—was probably a casualty of this collective disgust. It is worth quoting in detail as an illustration of the effect of an army intent on "giving South Carolina hell":

> *The interior of the mansion exhibited a confused scene. The most elegant description of furniture was found scattered about and broken, pianos and melodeons, a telescope, centre tables, costly chairs, ottomans, carpets, a fine collection of books and pictures and paintings, all scattered about in confusion and disorder. The troops after satisfying their curiosity and helping themselves to a book or picture from the deserted plantation, departed, and a few minutes after, the grand homestead of Dr. Bostic, together with its deserted contents, was in ashes, the chimneys alone remaining to mark another mile of country subjugated.*[52]

Such destruction was hardly unique. Williams's men put the town to the torch. A Wisconsin soldier witnessed the only home spared in an earlier rampage in flames as his regiment passed through. In a telling statement, the soldier went on to remark that it was "true all of our whole march through SC, that a house, not actually occupied was burned." This understanding, that unoccupied dwellings were "fair game," seems to have been at least tacitly accepted throughout Sherman's command. Occupied dwellings at least had the option of asking for a guard, which may or may not save the home. But in the words of one eyewitness, "it is a sad mistake that the people make when leaving their houses, for their property would not suffer near as much if they remained."[53]

Sherman himself would quip in a letter to Wheeler that his orders prohibited his men burning homes held by "peaceful families." Uncle Billy went on to insist that he believed these orders to be obeyed. But as for unoccupied dwellings that were "of no use to anybody," Sherman adopted an apathetic policy. If their owners didn't see fit to remain in their homes, Sherman did not care of the fate of the abandoned domiciles. Although Sherman softened his rhetoric by insisting that he did not desire any private homes be destroyed, his infuriatingly naïve assumption that his men were following orders and that Southern families could trust his rampaging army is perplexing. Sherman need only notice the pillars of smoke surrounding his columns and hear of frightful encounters by civilians to see evidence that brought his assumption into question.[54]

The destruction of Robertville was so complete that it is probably best to let the words of later witnesses tell the story. One soldier quipped after

South Carolina's greatest villain, Major General William T. Sherman. *Courtesy of the Library of Congress.*

passing through the ruins that it was a "very nice little village but now there is nothing left to mark the place except about one hundred 'monuments' (chimnies) erected to the memory of Jefferson D."[55] Colonel James C. Rodgers of the 123rd New York remarked that a "heap of ashes" was all that remained of the village, while one of his men noted only standing chimneys left behind.[56] Chillingly, a man of the regiment serenaded to give South Carolina hell, laconically described Robertville only as a "small place burned."[57] Hell had come to South Carolina, and many more "small places" would face a similar result.

The following day, Ward closed the gap. With the town seized, there still remained the difficulty of cutting through to Sister's Ferry. Selfridge's brigade had already run into difficulties at Cypress Creek. Unfortunately, his new route to the river would take him directly through the teeth of another portion of the same quagmire. Undeterred, Selfridge dispatched the 123rd New York and 5th Connecticut to push their way through. For the New Yorkers, stymied earlier, it was a chance to try again. Problems abounded from the very beginning, as the lone causeway was found completely submerged by the rising waters of Great Black Swamp. Selfridge's troops waded over a mile down the causeway before reaching the swollen waters of Cypress Creek, again. The rising torrent had once again ripped away the bridge.[58]

With no other options, Selfridge's men downed a tree across with the understated "good deal of difficulty." The problems didn't end there, as Selfridge was only able to cross over a single company. The vanguard sank waist deep into the swamp until solid ground finally emerged. No doubt providing an interesting sight, the drenched detail finally reached the ferry. A strong work party and guard were left to construct two footbridges through the frigid morass throughout the night and following day. For some, the work continued.

Footbridges in place, Selfridge pushed the 46th Pennsylvania and 141st New York through the knee-deep swamp to Sister's Ferry on January 30. There work began on a dock for unloading supplies. Thus, with a great deal of work and grit, Selfridge's brigade had secured Sister's Ferry. The following day, the remaining elements of Selfridge's command were ordered back through the quagmire to reach the landing.

Despite the relatively dry trip across the footbridges snaking over the creek, the causeway still remained submerged for over a mile. Thus, for a second straight day, Selfridge's men waded through the frigid water. For five companies of the 123rd New York, there was no comforting notion of drying their soaked possessions. The hard-luck band would be detached on a wild goose chase for Rebels a few miles above the landing.[59] At the landing, the brigade would temporarily stay as it prepared for the rest of the Left Wing.

That same day, January 31, Williams circulated a directive regarding indiscriminate pillaging of homes.[60] For the citizens of Robertville and Hardeeville, both present and in flight, it was a little too late. As villages and homes ahead would find, the order didn't seem worth the paper it was written on. For the next month, Federal troops would make the campaign famous for their path of destruction. South Carolina, the "Cradle of Secession," was about to see, as it had so far, hell on earth.

Chapter 5

Here Began a Carnival of Destruction

With plumes of smoke rising into the horizon as telltale signs of destruction, Confederates outside Union lines must have looked on with helplessness and befuddlement. If the destruction at Robertville and Hardeeville were any indication, these distant towers of smoke would be present as long as the Confederates were retreating. Until they could find a place to fight, the black smoke would continue from evacuated towns and homesteads.

This distressing realization in mind, the Confederate forces continued preparations. Lieutenant General Hardee placed McLaws's two-thousand-man division along the Salkehatchie River to delay Sherman along its black waters, while Wheeler's Cavalry corps screened Sherman's columns. Lieutenant Colonel Paul Anderson's one-hundred-man-strong Fourth Tennessee Cavalry manned such a post a half mile from McTier's Mill. At 10:00 a.m. on January 30, Anderson's pickets met the advance elements of the Right Wing.

Overpowered, Anderson's men yielded McTier's Mill Creek with little struggle. Anderson's scouts did manage to hover on the Federal column long enough to determine that this was not just another detachment. The Federals were busily repairing the destroyed bridge at McTier's, while artillery wheels and wagons rumbled nearby. The troopers stayed close enough to determine that this large force of the enemy was strung for several miles. Mere diversions were not known to travel this heavily.

Sherman's Right Wing was on the move. The Seventeenth Corps had advanced six miles from Pocotaligo and seized a position along the

Salkehatchie Road. Their move had also secured the junction of their own route with the road to McPhersonville. The Fifteenth Corps was rolling as well. Jumping off from positions near Gardens Corner and Port Royal Ferry, Major General John Logan's corps was in position on the outskirts of McPhersonville by nightfall on January 30. Sherman's Right Wing was nearly prepared to cut into the interior. However, the next day would see one last scrape as Federal troops kept up the scare.[61]

Two regiments of Brigadier General Manning Force's Third Division moved toward the Salkehatchie River railroad bridge. No stranger to the deadly zip of Rebel lead, Force snatched life from the jaws of death when he suffered a wound to the face at the Battle of Atlanta. Disfigured, the former Harvard-educated attorney now found himself once again in harm's way.[62] While a part of Force's men skirmished along the riverbank, more of their comrades took to felling trees. The bluff and bluster was as much about form as substance. Militarily, Force's afternoon show amounted to merely a demonstration, the sole object of the work being to feign a crossing.

Posted across the river, Lieutenant Colonel Stackhouse's South Carolina riflemen from Conner's brigade and artillery roared into action. However, the affair ended with little effect. In at least one respect, all the noise and hacking was more than just a show. Across the river, one of Stackhouse's men lay dead after a Yankee shot rang true.[63] Sadly, he would not be the last. More blood was on the way and soon.

On the morning of February 1, the Right Wing stepped off. Led by the Ninth Illinois Mounted Infantry, the Seventeenth Corps moved out toward Broxton's Bridge over the Salkehatchie. Shortly after leaving camp, the Illinoisans became the target of harassment by about six hundred Rebel horsemen. Engaged heavily, the mounted men pressed the Confederates back toward Whippy Swamp. Blair's column fought its way through, reaching its destination around midday. Their harassers swung up the left-hand road toward Crockettsville. Thanks to the Illinoisans, the Confederates barely came near Blair's main column. In all fairness, they scarcely could have made too much difference if they had gotten any closer.

Despite the comforting news, the Confederate turn had not left the road open. At Whippy Swamp, a squadron of the Third South Carolina Cavalry and a piece of horse artillery held a barricaded position across the swamp to slow Blair down. As usual, downed trees blocked the causeway, and its five bridges were burned. Far more formidable than the few barricaded Rebels, the swamp offered one of the first visual signs of the terrain to be found from now on in the Palmetto State. Describing such conditions, Right Wing commander Howard recalled:

> *There were pine woods everywhere—outside and in the swamps; and bordering the creeks we found the cypress trees, often very close together. Occasionally, wide stretches would appear like good ground, but prove on trial to be merely troublesome quicksands with a deceitful surface. Even along the roads, as our men said, "the bottom falls out" before many wagons have passed over, so that we quickly corduroyed by covering the surface with small pines. Thousands of men worked at this…passing through this sort of country, Confederate cavalry, now quite numerous, obstructed every causeway, held us in check as long as they could, and then destroyed the lagoon bridges before every column. Sometimes these bridges would be sixty or seventy feet long, and when burned caused much delay for replacement. Now and then the roads were filled with fallen timber for miles, entangling as the tree tops came together from each side of the road.*[64]

With his skirmishers pushed forward and at work, the Right Wing chief had scouting in mind as he and his entourage moved down to the swamp

"This sort of country": the quagmire of Whippy Swamp. *Courtesy of the author.*

for a better view. If Howard's party had any delusions that the Rebels would flee at the sight of anything blue, they were sadly mistaken. The stubborn Confederates across the swamp made no distinction between skirmisher and staff officers, directing some of their fire at Howard's party.

At least one of them aimed well. Immediately to Howard's rear, a ball struck Lieutenant William N. Taylor in the neck. The projectile passed to the inside of his main artery, cut his windpipe and emerged out in front of the main artery on his left side. Remarkably, the ball had missed both arteries. Howard grasped the young officer by the neck, preventing both blood and precious air from escaping his wound.[65] At the very least, the South Carolinians could claim to coming within a hairsbreadth of killing Howard, again, before inevitably being driven off. Howard nearly paid with his life for not learning from his near miss along Horspa Creek.

Major General Joseph Mower's First Division was charged with running off the Confederates. Mower was certainly one of the up-and-coming stars of Sherman's army. Regarded as "the boldest young soldier we have" by his "elder" Sherman, Uncle Billy thought enough of the Massachusetts native to offer him his own command should he kill the dreaded Nathan Bedford Forrest in battle and not receive his promised promotion. A former carpenter in his prearmy life, Mower combined his blue-collar work ethic with high rank.[66]

Mower was the type of commander who would just as soon wade into the swamp with his men as lead from the safety of the rear. Considering the drenched country ahead, this was just the kind of officer needed. Mower was his regular self at Whippy Swamp, throwing out the Eighteenth Missouri to push through.[67] As the Missourians forced their way through the cypress swamp, the outnumbered Rebels gave way. The routine yet deadly work now accomplished, Mower's pioneers cleared the road for the passage of his command that night. Besides Taylor, one other Federal was wounded that day.

The Fifteenth Corps was likewise ordered onward. Ahead was summer resort village McPhersonville. Like Robertville, McPhersonville bore the distinction of being one of the first planter-heavy villages greeting the Yankee invaders. Interestingly, the village owed its whole existence to the therapeutic—or, more accurately, preventive—qualities of the area. Faced with sickly summer months, many planters who lived in low-lying, mosquito-infested areas sought out pine-covered sites farther inland. These pine havens eventually spawned summer homes. As families carved out lots for their summer abodes, neighbors were gained, summer chapels began and bonds created as villages took root. The fine *History of Beaufort County* colossus captured the importance of these minisocieties by pronouncing the resort villages as "centers of white planter society just as the street was the center of the slave community."

McPhersonville was one of these villages.[68] General John McPherson and Congressman James Elliot McPherson built some of the first resort homes on the site. Families with plantations in Prince William Parish came to carve out their own slice of what would soon be called McPhersonville. A child of one of its native families, Dr. Louis McPherson DeSaussure recalled his neighbors as "unpretentious" but nevertheless did not shy away from reporting that they certainly would qualify as "well to do." Considering their planter roots, the modest description was no doubt a euphemism for a comfortable lifestyle among the pines.

By the "late unpleasantness," McPhersonville would seem to an observer doing all that it could to hide from the world as the village found itself cuddled in the pine forest's embrace. There the familiar pines and ridges so desired for summer resorts were in abundance. Despite the recent surge in prosperity and construction of the 1850s, the village still lay in the midst of its pine protectors on the eve of the Civil War.[69]

A soon-to-be-arrived Yankee of the 103rd Illinois scathingly described the village that seemingly had been swallowed up by the pines. Almost as if mocking the pretension of a village nestled away in woods like a setting from a Brothers Grimm storybook, McPhersonville was to him "quite a place, but there is not even a clearing. Say 50 ordinary dwellings dropped down in the pine woods, and you have it."[70] In a more sophisticated, overt condescension, another Northern soldier of the 12th Indiana remarked that the village tucked away in the vast pine forest was a "curious spectacle to eyes accustomed of beauty and fertility in the vicinity of rural villages of the North."[71]

As the Fifteenth Corps closed upon McPhersonville, a sinister correspondence became prophetic. In 1864, Union general Henry Halleck made a cryptic but unmistakable allusion to antiquity in a letter to the instrument of his wrath, Sherman. Like Roman soldiers of yesteryear's yesteryear at Carthage, Halleck looked on in rage at the Confederacy, which had kept the Union engrossed in war for nearly four years. And amid it all, the birthplace of secession, Charleston, sat defenseless.

With Charleston ripe for the picking, Halleck saw to it that Sherman would not let such a prize go without punishment. Correspondence to Sherman dripped with an ire more suited for the Inquisition than from an officer of the American republic. Viewing Charleston as if it was a heretical bastion in a holy crusade, Halleck chillingly requested that "by some accident" Charleston be destroyed. Alluding to Rome's desolation of Carthage, the erudite Halleck opined that "if a little salt should be sown upon its site it may prevent the growth of future crops of nullification and secession." It was quite an interesting opinion for a man who had authored a treatise in May 1861 on just how far was too far in waging war.[72]

In a less than flattering moment that does little justice to his arguably embellished image as a "lover of the south," Sherman matched Halleck's suggestion, venom for venom. Sherman reminded the chief of staff that salt would be hardly necessary. After all, his own Fifteenth Corps would make up his right flank. This would, Sherman replied, place them as the force entering Charleston. Sherman, by his own admission, was fully confident that they would continue to "do their work up pretty well."[73] Unfortunately, "good work" would be defined as a wrecked birthplace of secession. Ironically, Sherman had once been stationed in Charleston while a young U.S. Army officer. If he had forgotten those youthful days, he would shortly have a friendly reminder at Orangeburg.

As fate would have it, none of Sherman's army would ravage Charleston. But the promise of the Fifteenth Corps as an instrument of wrath still manifested itself. As fires later raged in Columbia, Sherman's remark to Halleck took on a much more sinister hue. Even before that terrible night of fires that began under the Fifteenth Corps's watch (its culprits a widely debated question), McPhersonville lay directly in the path of the men whose own commander promised to wreck Charleston.

On January 30, the Fifteenth Corps stepped off en route to the village. What greeted them was a deserted countryside. A man of the Ninety-third Illinois recalled seeing no citizen on the march from Beaufort. In a twisted justification, the charred remnants of "nearly every house" along their route was justified by their being "dilapidated concerns." It was a harrowing prescience that would resurface throughout the next two weeks as the same soldier recalled that all of the burned homes were abandoned. In this they had committed what was often an unpardonable sin.[74] Many would be introduced to the flames as penance.

As the advance elements of Brigadier General Charles Woods's First Division stormed into McPhersonville, they found it as deserted as those "dilapidated concerns" along their march. Moses D. Gage of the 12th Indiana found no white inhabitants left in the village. A comrade in the 103rd Illinois went so far as to extend the desertion to both the white and black dwellers.

McPhersonville was empty. An empty village it was and completely at the mercy of its conquerors.

Military order apparently prevailed early on—to a degree. The first Yankees in the hamlet soon figured out more about it and its absent tenants. The fact that the village was a summer haven for rich planters was not lost on at least some of the rank and file of Woods's division. The previously mentioned Gage noted that the more prosperous citizens of the village were planters from the nearby river bottoms. Another occupier found tangible proof of the village's blue-blooded origins just by the content of the homes when he recollected, "this place was a summer resort…the room was filled with mahogany furniture of the best quality, had a fine piano, splendid plate mirror, and a fine library."[75]

Thus, McPhersonville gave little reason for sympathy from Sherman's men; the wealth of the inhabitants was on display for all to see. As such, the midwesterners kicking in doors of the deserted village had little appreciation for the planters' need to be surrounded by their finest during their summer exodus. Opulence that helped make for a happy, comfortable home in peacetime could provide quite the impetus for rage in the turbulent fourth year of a bitter war.

If faithful adherence to luxurious living didn't arouse the ire of the Federal occupiers, there were, of course, the remnants of the village's role as a Confederate military post. The Prince William Parish Episcopal summer chapel still remained as the impromptu smallpox hospital during those early Confederate days. More tangible was a scrap of Confederate correspondence found in a vacant building by some traipsing Federals. Although undated, the substance of the letter suggested it to be a holdover from McPhersonville's martial past. It must have been delightfully ironic for its discoverers to read an abandoned treatise on defending the very ground they now stood on.

Finally, a blip of Rebel resistance showed that Confederate cavalry still roamed. Small bands of Rebels harassed the roads leading toward Pocotaligo. At least one wagon was captured and a man's horse shot dead, leaving a few Federal officers to wonder how Rebels were located several miles in their rear. More perplexing was how difficult it would be to identify these Rebels since they deceptively wore Yankee blue. The bands had little effect on the Union efforts, but at the very least they were a reminder that the army's rear was not safe for unescorted wagon trains as long as Confederate cavalry roamed.[76]

Regardless of peripheral affairs, McPhersonville's natives had committed an unforgivable, though understandable, sin of neglect. The words of our aforementioned diarist Gage come back hauntingly. The abandoned village left little moral justification to the enraged occupiers to protect it. Abandoned by its owners, the trespassing Yankees passed the night of January 30 and the following day doing little collateral damage beyond pillaging. Some even made use of the Stony Creek Independent Presbyterian Church for a worship service.

Along with the Prince William Parish Episcopal Church, Stony Creek Independent Presbyterian Church was the "city on a hilltop" in McPhersonville. These two houses of worship were where the spiritual needs of the McPhersonville village were met. Predictably, both churches were the summer chapels of existing churches. Stony Creek was the satellite church of the Independent Presbyterian Church of Stony Creek. Founded in 1743 near Pocotaligo, the "mother church" drew its coffers from the local planters of indigo, cotton and rice in the area.[77] It was this church that was destroyed by Federals near Stony Creek days earlier. Its summer chapel in McPhersonville was finished in 1833.

Whatever praises and acclamations of New Testament Christian love may have come forth within the walls of the little white churches, Yankees engaged in an assault on the village straight out of an Old Testament prophecy. "The houses and furniture of the wealthier citizens were left to their fate," recalled a Union soldier in the orgy of destruction.[78] Laconic as they may be, his words need little embellishment. No doubt the hamlet was ransacked by Union soldiers, with them stealing everything that could be had and destroying what couldn't be carried off. In the words of a soldier of the Ninetieth Illinois, McPhersonville "shared the fate which the conduct of our men today seemed to threaten all of South Carolina." In a realization that made McPhersonville's destruction virtually inevitable, Fifteenth Corps division commander William Hazen almost apologetically noted the difficulties in restraining the men so far in the state:

> No sooner had we passed Pocotaligo than the demon of destruction seized possession of everybody...South Carolina had fired the first gun and even the smallest drummer boy wanted to get even...We were not out of sight of Port Royal Ferry when the black columns of smoke began to ascend...Here began a carnival of destruction that ended with the burning of Columbia.[79]

The carnival of destruction in McPhersonville extended beyond mere looting, as the village was put to the torch. The thorough destruction was so complete that only a single church remains of the village to this day. Like

Stony Creek Independent Presbyterian Church is the only thing that remains of McPhersonville. *Courtesy of the author.*

a lone fence post in a long-abandoned field, the Stony Creek Independent Presbyterian Church summer chapel still marks what was McPhersonville. The Fifteenth Corps had certainly done their "work well" by the standards of the vengeful mood that seemed disturbingly prevalent in the army. The following day, Alonzo Brown of the Fourth Minnesota gave a chilling premonition of more to come as the Yankees were ready to "teach South Carolina the lesson she deserves."[80] Thus, the fate of McPhersonville would not be an isolated occurrence.

On February 1, the Fifteenth Corps continued toward Hickory Hill. Trying to block future destruction was much of the same opposition that greeted Blair's corps. Dismounted Rebel horsemen downed trees and harassed Logan's column from the protection of barricades. The nipping Confederate troopers would have no more success than their comrades harassing the Seventeenth Corps. Logan's Seventh Illinois and Twenty-ninth Missouri struck hard and had little trouble slugging back the small brigade of Rebel cavalry. The First Division had the lead and reached Hickory Hill that same day.

Despite the successful march, greeting Logan at Hickory Hill was a regiment of Confederate cavalry drawn up on the opposite side of the river.

The force had stout outposts posted on the causeway and bridge. These barricades threatened to expose the Yankees to concentrated fire as they passed down the narrow causeway. For the first time, Confederate horsemen had the opportunity to avenge the black smoke in the distance that was once McPhersonville.

Fittingly, Woods's First Division, so prominent at McPhersonville, came to blows with the Rebel troopers. Brigadier General William Woods's First Brigade received the call to clear the way. In a prelude to the brand of fighting to come, Woods threw out his men in a line of battle to uproot the Confederates. What he soon discovered was that the defenders had terrain on their side. The river flowed through a milewide dense cypress swamp with waters reaching waist deep. Behind this natural abatis, the Southern horsemen showed signs of making a stand.

Woods decided to push only his skirmishers through the mess ahead. The Yankee men worked their way doggedly through the watery impediment. Fighting both the swamp and fervent musketry, the Federals drove the game but overwhelmed Rebels from the opposite bank. However, the sharp fighting had wounded a man of the Ninth Iowa in the thigh, forcing the amputation of his leg.[81] Personal accounts noted one cavalryman was killed and another wounded in the advance, presumably in the skirmishing leading up to Hickory Hill. Another claims two died in the fighting. Whatever the casualties, for at least a few Union soldiers, their part in McPhersonville's desolation had been returned in kind.

The sharp fight did not remove Yankee friskiness, as Logan's vandals overran a nearby residence. Its owner, Mrs. McBride, had already fled. Not surprisingly, the flight had opened up her home to a guiltless rampage by Sherman's men and their apathetic officers. Even Sherman's presence did little to ward off abuses, as the outhouses were soon in flames. A Yankee chaplain recalled the chieftain had barely climbed into his saddle before flames consumed the widow's house. In a sign of things to come, orders for such burnings were not given, but assistance to arrest such behavior seemed disturbingly few and far between.[82]

Elements of Logan's mounted infantry were ordered to the Sister's Ferry Road's crossing of the Coosawhatchie Swamp to save the bridge for use by Corse's Fourth Division. Withdrawing Rebel cavalry stopped long enough to partially destroy the bridge, giving Corse's men reason to later lament this seemingly trivial development.[83] At any rate, most of the Fifteenth Corps was up and concentrated.[84] The day had seen both blood and destruction. The campaign was already unfolding as expected.

Chapter 6

Men Gasping in Death

The Right Wing was steamrolling ahead, and there seemed to be little the Confederates could do as it snaked along the narrow roads between the Coosawhatchie and Salkehatchie Rivers. To their south, the Twentieth Corps was slugging through their own share of swamps. It could be expected that eventually the Confederates would finally regain their old vigor and take vengeance, but when and where remained to be seen.

Concentrated near Robertville, the Twentieth Corps had connected with the landing at Sister's Ferry by the end of January. From there would come the estranged Fifteenth and Twentieth Corps Divisions. Equally important, the crossing would finally bring over the Fourteenth Corps and Judson Kilpatrick's cavalry division to join Sherman's forces in South Carolina. This event would mean the reuniting of Sherman's entire command in the Palmetto State.

However, it would be over a week before Left Wing commander Major General Henry Slocum's other corps began moving into the state. First, Slocum's men had to construct a pontoon bridge, which was completed on January 29. The bridge was the easy part of their task. For the next six days, Slocum's men corduroyed roads, built bridges and removed obstacles emplaced by the desperate Rebels.

That much of the flooding had inundated the roadway only complicated matters. As they had at Fort McAllister near Savannah, Georgia, crafty Rebels left a surprise. Torpedoes or land mines exploded along the road, killing and wounding several of Slocum's men.[85] With

Major General
Henry Slocum,
Left Wing
commander.
*Courtesy of the
Library of Congress.*

deadly impediments such as these, Slocum's crossing would take time.
But while Slocum's men worked constantly, Federals already in South
Carolina were on the move again.

Slocum's delay across the Savannah was not far from Sherman's mind
during these early days. Sherman did not want his Right Wing to outdistance
itself from its Left Wing counterpart. With time to spare, Howard altered the
original order to march his Fifteenth Corps directly to Angley's post office.
Instead, the Fifteenth Corps would move via the lower route at Duck Creek.
This could give Slocum more time to cross and close the gap between the
two wings. Slocum's command would need only to march via Lawtonville to
the Duck Branch post office to connect with the Fifteenth Corps. However,
Sherman clearly was not intending to wait long for his Left Wing and accepted
that he may have to move to the South Carolina Railroad without them.[86]

With Major General William Hazen's Second Division as the advance,
the Fifteenth Corps resumed their march on February 2 toward Loper's
Crossroads and Duck Creek. A Vermont native transplanted to Ohio at an

46

early age, Hazen struck up a friendship in his younger years with fellow Union soldier, senator and future president James A. Garfield. Just two years before the war, Hazen was badly wounded in a skirmish with the Comanches out West.[87] Neither of these notables mattered much in the cypress bottomlands he now found himself in. More pertinent for Hazen were more practical matters like expediently moving his division along. As the lead division, Hazen would not have to worry about delays ahead. Hazen had complained previously about the division preceding his own in the previous day's advance.[88] Today was a new day, and Hazen would usher it in.

Not helping matters was another bad stretch of road inundated in places with water "up to a horses belly and two or three hundred yards across."[89] More annoying than slow-footed comrades and the deluged swamplands, the Rebels ahead had not yet run. Once again, elements of Wheeler's cavalry waited at every creek and swamp crossing behind barricades and fallen timber. And like the day before, the Federal column had to devote some manpower to brush them out of the way. Colonel Theodore Jones's First Brigade bore the brunt of the fighting, striking the Rebels at two o'clock that afternoon. The Sixth Missouri and Thirtieth Ohio drove the Confederates back in a fight that lasted until dark. The overwhelmed Rebel troopers fell back to safety across Duck Creek.

The day's fighting had not been without heartache, as two Rebels were killed. For the Federals, three men of the Sixth Missouri and two of the Thirtieth Ohio were wounded. The poor roads did prove to be the Southerners' best friend, as it kept the First and Third Divisions from reaching Loper's Crossroads, forcing them into camp four miles back. It had been a fifteen-mile march.[90] At least Hazen could take solace in the fact that this time he was not among those lagging behind.

Signs were all around of the chivalry, even if they themselves were absent. War correspondent David Conyngham noted the fine plantations lining the roads. Though they were well provisioned with supplies, their owners had taken the "French leave." Another common staple was prevalent, as many shared the fate of the unfortunate Mrs. McBride's residence—the torch. A correspondent in the First Michigan Engineers recalled this usual business as he noted for posterity "several fine houses were set fire to and burned."

As Mr. Conyngham seconded with refreshing candor:

> *If a house was empty, this was prima facie evidence that the owners were*
> *Rebels, and all was sure to be consigned to the flames. If they remained*
> *at home, it was taken for granted that every one in South Carolina was a*

Rebel, and the chances were the place was consumed...few escaped; and the country was converted into one vast bonfire.

Amid the devastation, Conyngham recalled Hazen and Sherman noticing a column of smoke ahead. Despondent, Hazen quipped, "There goes the bridge." After a few minutes, Sherman reassured him, "No, Hazen, no, that's a house; it is not the bridge. A bridge would not emit such dense smoke." It is difficult to discern what is more telling: the quickness with which Sherman could tell the difference or the callous regard he held for the burning of yet another home.[91] At the very least Sherman understandably was far more concerned with the bridges over the swollen Carolina swamps than another home resigned to the flames. This preoccupation with burning bridges in the midst of collateral destruction is a telling microcosm of the campaign to date.

While Logan's corps operated near Duck Creek, the Seventeenth Corps resumed their advance on February 2. Force's Third Division was ordered up the left-hand road to Angley's post office. The Ninth Illinois Mounted Infantry would be their vanguard up to that point, where the mounted men would then swing back toward the remainder of the corps. While Force's division was away, the First and Fourth Divisions would move on Broxton's Bridge over the Salkehatchie River.

Despite its natural advantages, the Confederates offered only McLaws's two thousand men to guard the Salkehatchie. This in mind, the Georgian stretched his division into place along its three major crossings. The southeasternmost in the line was Broxton's Bridge. Stretching about five miles upstream, one would come to the crossing at Rivers' Bridge. Even farther upstream was Buford's Bridge. It was these three crossings that would make up the Salkehatchie line. For both Rebel and Yankee alike, February 2 offered all the inklings of an impending fight. If inklings failed them, Sherman offered a hint of his own. In a warning to Howard, Sherman remarked, "At Rivers' you will find infantry and artillery in position."[92] The next two days would prove just how ominously prophetic such words would be.

That morning, Mower's First Division again had the advance. Four companies of skirmishers from the Twenty-fifth Indiana of Colonel John Tillson's Third Brigade groped along for Confederates blocking the way. They did not have long to wait. A mile and a half from camp, the skirmishers struck Rebel cavalry. Along the Federal column, the crackle of musketry gave promise of either a coming "fight" or just a rehashing of the slight skirmishing leading to Whippy Swamp. To all concerned, it would seem the latter was the case, as the Hoosiers drove back the Southerners. Once again, Yankees were moving forward with Rebel horsemen clopping away in retreat. For smug Yankees, once again the chivalry had been met and easily dispatched in South Carolina.

Outnumbered again, the troopers tried all they could to keep back Tillson's skirmishers, even attempting to gain their flank with a sudden charge. However, the Yankee rifles countered such pluck, emptying a few saddles. There was no stopping the Yankees as they slugged the Rebels across Broxton's Bridge. By Blair's order, the Twenty-fifth Indiana held up. The Rebels had prepared the position well with infantry entrenched in a redoubt and the bridge burned. Mainly interested in giving plenty of bark with little bite, the Hoosiers stayed behind to keep the Confederates at Broxton's Bridge occupied.

With the Twenty-fifth Indiana keeping up the scare, the rest of Mower's column swung up the road leading to Rivers' Bridge. Leading the advance party of the Ninth Illinois Mounted Infantry was Lieutenant Colonel Dennis T. Kirby of Blair's staff.[93] Kirby's detachment had not long to wait before barricaded Rebel horsemen were again found. Undeterred, the Yankees pitched in with their usual fury. If the Confederates expected any less vigor, they were sadly mistaken. Once again, they yielded ground. In fact, for three miles the Southerners were forced back. However, the Rebels' passive nature would shortly end.

The Rebels reined in behind a barricade and dug in their heels to hold their ground with unusual stubbornness. It was a position far more advantageous than the others. Swamps bordered each flank, while an open field stretched along the front. It was the perfect place for a defense, allowing defenders to completely command the ground over which the Yankees would attack while their flanks lay secure. Throwing out skirmishers, Kirby charged the barricaded secessionists.

The defenders waited for their foes to be on top of them before breaking before the combined charge.[94] With such audacity, however, there is always a cost, as a ball found Kirby. The round cut through his calf, killing the unfortunate beast he was riding. With the skirmishers of the Thirty-second Wisconsin now out front and pressing the Rebel front, the mounted infantry worked its once more open flanks. Plenty of firepower on hand, the Yankees were able to overpower the stubborn troopers and seize the Buford's Bridge–Rivers' Bridge crossroad. To keep up the scare at Buford's Bridge, Mower pushed Tillson's brigade a half a mile up in that direction. Feigning both on Broxton's and Buford's Bridge, Mower now turned his column on Rivers' Bridge.

Colonel Milton Montgomery's Second Brigade now led the column. A battalion of the Twenty-fifth Wisconsin advanced as skirmishers toward the crossing. Striking a Rebel outpost along the causeway, the battalion made short work of the Rebel pickets, sending them off in hasty retreat. In fact, the Wisconsin men drove with such vigor that the Rebels neglected to burn the valuable causeway bridges over the swamp. In a fiefdom of swamps, bridges are king. The retiring Rebels did set fire to the bridge over the Salkehatchie. Watching his comrades flushed back like a flock of birds from a bush, Confederate soldier Benjamin Williams recounted the battle's early moments: "They came in (the vedettes) closely followed by the enemy. Indeed so closely pressed that it was with difficulty that the bridges could be destroyed after our men had crossed, the latter part of the work being done under a galling fire from the enemy."[95]

Flushed with easy success, the Yankees kept moving. However, an unusual arrangement offered a deadly surprise for the onrushing skirmishers. About three quarters of a mile from the crossing, the causeway made an abrupt turn to the left. As the Federals made this dogleg turn leading to the last section of road, the crossing came into view. Unfortunately for Montgomery's skirmishers, their early success was misleading.

At the end of the road and on a low hill across the river, earthworks completely commanded the causeway from its dogleg turn to the river.[96] Along with four emplaced artillery pieces, about eight hundred rifles lay ahead. The Confederates, who had run for two days, finally showed defiance. As Yankees came into range along the road, artillerymen of Earle's Battery, Company A, Palmetto Battalion, South Carolina Light Artillery opened fire on the invaders of their native soil. The chivalry had stopped running.

In the breastworks ahead the rifles of the Thirty-second and Forty-seventh Georgia under Lieutenant Colonel Edwin Bacon erupted. A few companies of the Third South Carolina Cavalry dismounted to help in the developing fight. Among them was John B. Woods, blood draining from his leg wounded by a Yankee ball. By morning, Woods had lost too much blood, and the life of the "good soldier" memorialized as dependable in any emergency had ended.[97]

The Rebel artillery continued its deadly effect as a Wisconsin sergeant and bugler were struck down, the latter decapitated.[98] The Federals pushed as far as the river before being halted by the withering fire. Finding themselves the focal point of every piece of lead emanating from the breastworks, a few more of the Wisconsin men collapsed, two of them fatally. The Rebel

The end of the line: the Salkehatchie River crossing at Rivers' Bridge. *Courtesy of the author.*

fire was too heavy to go on. The Rebel tenacity so absent since Atlanta had finally returned.

Along the causeway, Federals prudently threw themselves into its surrounding swamps while the balance of Montgomery's brigade filed into position. Rebel artillery remained up to its frisky business. An indiscriminate assassin, the guns made even the lofty their targets. While deploying the Forty-third Ohio into line, a shell fragment struck former Medal of Honor winner Colonel Wager Swayne, who required an amputation. One of his men fared no better, struck down with wounds. Another shell nearly scored a coup as it made a direct beeline for Mower as he surveyed the scene. Only a last-second leap backward saved him as the shell exploded in his hastily evacuated spot.[99]

The guns had their most devastating effect for any Federals foolishly caught on the causeway. The battery fired directly down the straight stretch of road from the angle to the earthworks, placing any person along the causeway in mortal danger. Eyewitness Major Thomas Osborn did notice at least one fortunate turn in the disposition of the

Confederate artillery. In Osborn's eyes, the guns could have been even more dangerous had they swept in an arc to include the road on the opposite side of the angle.[100]

The souls of the mangled dead, cries of the wounded and Franklin Lesh of the Sixty-third Ohio would disagree with Osborn's assessment. Lesh recalled the road's layout allowing Rebel gunners to "see and kill" some of their men on the causeway. If he needed any other visceral proof, Lesh recalled vividly the "dreadful" wound of a man he helped drag from the swamp. The unfortunate Union sergeant had one side of his head shot away.[101] Regardless of their alleged inadequacies, the Confederate defenses had stopped Mower's advance cold.

The jockeying was not without other difficulties. A soldier of the Thirty-second Ohio recalled the Salkehatchie's forbidding swamps as "ranging from knee to waist deep, full of fallen trees, cypress vines, and deep holes, which with the tangled underbrush and vines that grew between, made anything but pleasant marching."[102] If it was not the threat of unseen, submerged holes that snatched men into the swamp's grip, every wounded man stood the risk of drowning, as he lay in the swamp's deep bottoms.

Because of the sudden Confederate defiance, the crossing of the Salkehatchie would have to wait. The rest of the afternoon would be filled with the sounds of musketry and crash of the four Rebel guns. Federal skirmishers used whatever cover could be found; however, the first day of fighting at Rivers' Bridge settled down into an inconclusive firefight. The cooling of the situation must have sat fine with Right Wing commander Howard. The veteran officer would refer to Rivers' Bridge as "the strongest position I have ever seen."

Leaving behind a heavy skirmish line, Mower withdrew from the swamp. With fresh orders to force the crossing the following day, Mower knew it would take some maneuvering to find a way around the Confederate roadblock. The Rebel works had been built with the sole purpose of blocking the bridge crossing. Any attack up the causeway would be doomed to heavy casualties. The Rebel flank would have to be found and rolled up.

During the night, Federal pioneers went to work cutting a road through the swamp. While they worked, skirmisher fire continued. Some Yankees even threw up a rifle pit to harass the troublesome Rebel batteries. Despite the festivities, the Confederates had been having their wish so far. Lieutenant Colonel Bacon had previously remarked to a superior that he could "hold the position until Christmas if you can keep them off my flanks." Another Confederate recalled fearing a flank attack more than a frontal assault. The weakness to the position was its vulnerable flanks, and the Georgians knew it. As for now, the Yankees had yet to find them.

The following morning came quickly enough. As daylight crept through the dense swamps, Mower had his men already at work. In testament to the frigid previous night, Mower's men found themselves breaking ice from their coats. This would be just one of many times that Federals moving through the South Carolina swamps would leave with uniforms frozen stiff. Regardless of the disagreeable weather, there was only one way out of the icy hell. Mower and his men would have to hack, wade and fight their way out.

Difficulties and all, it was time to put the plan to breach the Salkehatchie to work. Mower ordered Tillson's brigade into the swamp. The Tenth Illinois was thrown to the right of the causeway and the Thirty-second Wisconsin and Twenty-fifth Indiana (since relieved from Broxton's Bridge) to its left. Montgomery and Fuller's brigades went to work building a road through the morass while those not pioneering were ordered to camp in readiness to support a breach.[103]

Colonel Tillson slowly pushed his men through. Each foot of ground wore on the men as the ankle-hugging mud and cohesion-breaking undergrowth slowed their progress. Finally after a half a mile, Tillson's men reached the riverbank. What greeted them were signs of more difficulty ahead. The river seemed to move in three distinct channels. More perilously, the Rebel earthworks opened upon them with a close, hot fire. Earlier that day, the "16 year old boys" of the Fifth Georgia Reserves and a couple of regiments of Wheeler's cavalry had reinforced the Southerners. In all, at least 1,200 Confederate rifles now defended Rivers' Bridge.

Trying to keep the Rebel artillery from another day of deadly shelling, Tillson ordered fifteen picked men to man the previously constructed rifle pit in the swamp. The convenient position, only two hundred yards' distance, provided a protected place to harass the gunners across the river. It was one of these fifteen rifles that wounded two men and killed another of the battery.[104] One of the embattled Carolinian gunners, W.M. Larke, recalled one Yankee sharpshooter dropping all three of his comrades from behind a log "20 to 30 steps" away. After a couple of near misses, Larke borrowed a rifle and dispatched the game Union sharpshooter.[105]

The enemy gunners kept honest, Tillson pushed three companies of the Thirty-second Wisconsin ahead to force the channels of the Salkehatchie. Three more companies were soon added, and Tillson's skirmishers pushed on. Wading through waist-deep water, crossing falling logs and battling the dense undergrowth, the Yankees slowly forced their will

The swamps of the "ugly black Salkehatchie." *Courtesy of the author.*

on the Salkehatchie. Close and concentrated Confederate fire from the earthworks continued to drop Federals. Likely not far from the Georgians' minds was that these were the men who had ravaged their beloved Georgia and promised more of the same for South Carolina. The "Ugly, Black" Salkehatchie and a valiant band of Confederates were trying their best to hold back the equally bold invaders.

By 12:00 p.m., Federals had finally forced their way across the third channel. The commander of the skirmish line, Lieutenant Colonel Carleson, asked for reinforcements, and the remaining three companies of the regiment were sent to his aid. This placed the entire Thirty-second Wisconsin across the river at a point eight hundred yards above the Confederate right flank. Tillson continued feeding men into the breach, funneling the Twenty-fifth Indiana across the river. Tillson's entire brigade, minus the Tenth Illinois, was now across the Salkehatchie.

Around 2:00 p.m., Mower ordered Montgomery and Fuller's brigades into the breach. However, the seeds of a controversy would be planted. Receiving the orders, Fuller asked whether he should form on Tillson's left after crossing. Mower's aide responded for Fuller to "use his own judgment" but added that General Mower wanted the enemy driven as rapidly as possible. In regard to the former, Fuller was in full compliance.

Meanwhile, to divert attention from the promising flank attack, Mower ordered Captain David Gillespie of the Tenth Illinois against the Confederate left. Earlier, Gillespie had expressed confidence that his men could force their way across. For the entrenched Georgians in their front, such confidence would be music to their ears. Captain Ephraim Wilson's company was the first to spring onto a fallen log to cross, giving him a vivid view of the "good Third Brigade skirmish":

> As soon as the tree was cut, I sprang upon it and crossed and ordered the men to follow...while we were crossing grape and canister, small shot and minie balls flew thick and fast, but no one up to this time had been hit…in a moment our whole company was safely over, in another they were deployed as skirmishers and were engaging the enemy fiercely.

Only one more company crossed before the deluge of fire stopped them cold. The two companies had no choice but to go to ground and keep up their fire until heavy musketry on their left cued them to move again. For Wilson, the lottery of lead flying through the air eventually found him: "I had only fairly got my company deployed and nicely to work when bang! I got it in the neck and fell to my knees in water to my waist." Risking bleeding to death or drowning in the swamp, Wilson slinked back to the rear on the same well-targeted log that brought him over, dodging lead and risking drowning in the river should he fall. Surviving the crossing, Wilson was not out of the "water" yet. Waist- and knee-deep water awaited him as he desperately waded the swamp to find a field hospital.[106] With the help of one of his men, he arrived safely, badly weakened by leaving so much blood behind in the swamps. Such was warfare on the Salkehatchie.

With his mischief on the Confederate left stopped cold, Mower looked to Montgomery's brigade to continue to sway Confederate attention away from their endangered right flank. Unfortunately, there was only one place left to attack. The Forty-third Ohio and three companies of the Sixty-third Ohio were ordered straight up the causeway. This constituted a frontal assault up the same approach that Montgomery's men faced the day before. Fortunately for the hard-hit men of the Twenty-fifth Wisconsin, they wouldn't have to run the gauntlet again.

Mower's plan was to throw forward two companies at fixed bayonets on either side of the road as the first wave. Immediately behind them were

The swamps facing the Confederate left, Rivers' Bridge. *Courtesy of the author.*

two more companies carrying planking. The balance of the force followed. With the first wave providing covering fire, the second wave would repair the bridge. Behind them, the rest would assault the works. Before throwing the men in, the impetuous Mower "with an oath" told some of the Ohioans not to stop until they were inside the Confederate works.[107]

Following in their comrades' footsteps, Montgomery's men gallantly carried out their virtual suicide assault. Like the Wisconsin men before them, the Ohioans' attack was doomed. The Rebel guns wrought havoc, with one shell killing three men outright and wounding two more of the Sixty-third Ohio. The devastating fire sent the men bailing into the swamp, convincing Major Horace Park of the Forty-third Ohio to order the men to go no farther, as it was "madness."[108] There was no surviving the concentrated gauntlet of fire ahead.

Montgomery's men were stopped in their tracks, and once again the hearts of Bacon's Georgians swelled as they watched Sherman's men stopped cold. Whatever they lacked in numbers, they certainly made up for with raw grit. Foolish as it was, Mower's diversionary attack was certainly his "style," according to one of his disgruntled colonels. Oscar Jackson of the Sixty-

The entrenched bluff at Rivers' Bridge, as seen from the causeway. *Courtesy of the author.*

third Ohio probably remembered those hot moments along the causeway as he toured a battlefield hospital after the battle. Sights of "men mutilated in every shape conceivable, groaning, begging for assistance and gasping in death," probably brought to mind just how dangerous Mower's aggressive philosophy was for his men along the Salkehatchie.

The balance of Montgomery's brigade ventured to the left to support the flanking attack. There Tillson was giving the Confederates all they wanted with more help coming. The skirmishers were still in a lively firefight with the Rebels, eventually exhausting their ammunition. Upon arriving, the Twenty-fifth Indiana was fed into line. Rearmed with reinforcements, the line moved two hundred yards, all the while driving back the Confederate skirmishers. The Federals had found the Confederate right flank, and they were slowly rolling it up.

Tillson was gaining ground, but there was a cost. The occasional cry of men being struck and the wounded shuffling through the lines were evidence of the high price paid. Occasionally, men fell from a fatal blow. Others faced a possible death sentence as they collapsed into the water wounded. The soon-to-be-stunned Oscar Jackson would shortly recall the heads of some of the wounded propped up to prevent the immobilized men from drowning. Frightfully, Jackson suspected many wounded in the swamp would likely spend all night there, as finding and removing them would be impossible.[109]

About this time, Fuller arrived on the scene and quickly pulled rank on Tillson. Although both were brigade commanders, Fuller was a brigadier general to Tillson's rank of colonel. Having rank and fully willing to use it, Fuller ordered Tillson to halt his command while his own brigade formed on Tillson's flank. After learning of dry land ahead and Mower's orders to advance, Tillson rolled on again without his newly arrived superior. Fuller, who was still waiting on Montgomery's brigade to dress on his line, was forced to push after his advancing "subordinate." Fuller's plan to unite Mower's division for a combined thrust would have to wait.

While the war of wills between the two officers transpired, the Confederates were learning of the folly of staying around. At 3:00 p.m., McLaws ordered Colonel Bacon to try and hold until night and save his artillery. As the sound of heavy fire above and below their position filtered into the late afternoon hours, it must have felt as if the Federals would overwhelm their line at any time. The time had come to retreat.

With a skirmish line covering their right flank, the Confederates opened fire with heavy volleys of rifle and artillery from the entrenchments. In the smokescreen, they abandoned their works.[110] Their undermanned ranks had given as well as they had taken. They had held up a division of Sherman's troops led by one of his most aggressive commanders for a day and a half. However, military expediency now took precedence over valor. McLaws's division would totally abandon the Salkehatchie that night.

With nightfall fast approaching, Tillson's command bounded forward once again. Overwhelmed, the Rebel rear guard fell back steadily. Eventually, Fuller did finally come abreast of Tillson. Fuller slowed up Tillson's unilateral movements and waited until Montgomery's brigade arrived to advance again. As Mower arrived on the scene, Tillson was ordered forward once again, the rest of the division eventually following. Swarming the earthworks, Tillson's men found the familiar boys of the Tenth Illinois. After the Confederates slipped away, its stymied men hastened forward and seized the abandoned works. At least Captain Wilson's deadly track through the swamps was not in vain.

For one tardy detachment of the Third South Carolina Cavalry, the retreat was not so orderly. Riding into a group of Yankees, two of the men were captured. Two more made a break from the trap amid Yankee gunfire. Once they had reached safely, one man's rolled-up blanket and haversack

"The strongest position I have ever seen": the earthworks at Rivers' Bridge. *Courtesy of the author.*

contained balls intended for their fleeing owner. In the latter case, a pair of woolen gloves was all that prevented the ball from ripping through the haversack and into the soldier's hip.[111]

Mower's crossing was not the only success story along the Salkehatchie. Simultaneously, Major General Giles A. Smith's Fourth Division was ordered to cross between Broxton's and Rivers' Bridges. By the evening of February 3, Smith's division had forced its way across downstream of Rivers' Bridge after slight resistance. The Seventeenth Corps was now across the Salkehatchie in two places on either flank of the Rivers' Bridge defenders.

The "Battle" of Rivers' Bridge was over. The Federals had suffered heavily for the fighting involved. Colonel Tillson's brigade bore the brunt of casualties with 9 dead and 76 wounded. Colonel Montgomery, whose brigade had been primarily engaged in the "madness" along the causeway, suffered 9 killed and 23 wounded. Fuller had only 8 wounded. The final Federal casualties were along the lines of 18 dead and 107 wounded (6 mortally). Conversely, the Rebels suffered 10 dead, 45 wounded and 44 captured. Most of the Confederate casualties were left on the field.[112]

Over a week later, one Yankee correspondent felt nothing but pity for the abandoned Confederate wounded. Left behind in a makeshift hospital, William Fletcher King described the wounded as being "without food, wounds undressed, and no one to care for them." Making for an even more agonizing stay, the poorly ventilated room was full of smoke as the despondent men lay on the floors, feeling abandoned by comrades and longing for the homes they may never see again.[113] In another touching anecdote, Benjamin Williams watched as Captain Joe Thompson of the Forty-seventh Georgia was struck in the left side of his face by a ball. Left for dead by comrades, Williams would be shocked months later when his trip to pay respects to the deceased man's father brought him face to face with his "dead" comrade. Though badly disfigured, the captain had been moved—alive—to safety just before the retreat.[114]

At least two of the captured Rebels found themselves in quite an awkward situation. These two "galvanized" Rebels had been captured as Federals earlier in the war. Perhaps to spare themselves the hell of a Confederate prison, they had enlisted in the Thirty-second Georgia.[115] History does not record whether it was fear or joy that filled their hearts as they saw their old comrades swarm the Rebel lines.

Meanwhile, Force's Third Division saw action on February 2. Force's most troublesome resistance was found along the left bank of Whippy Swamp, with Corker's Swamp and several of its smaller neighbors slowing the passage of his wagons considerably. While his main column sloshed through the mud, Force ordered the Twentieth Illinois Mounted Infantry under Captain Munson up the road. Perhaps they would be enough to clear out any Rebels ahead while the column plodded along.

Early indications would suggest yes. Munson's command struck Rebel cavalry and drove them back to the crossing of Whippy Swamp at Barker's Mill. Fleeing across the bridge, the Rebel horsemen took position on a slight rise and in a grove. This new barrier stopped Munson, but the Rebels had been unable to accomplish an objective far greater than stalling a regiment of Federal horsemen. Their hasty flight left the bridge unburned.

Back up the road, Force found most of his trains had finally passed the swamps. Leaving the Twelfth Wisconsin and Forty-fifth Illinois to secure them, Force rode ahead to Barker's Mill. His advance unit followed right behind as extra muscle. On the scene, Force found Munson's men commanding the unburned bridge and preventing any Rebel foray to torch it. Behind Force, the advance arrived, spreading out on either side of the bridge as sharpshooters.

Force waited on the arrival of his main column before breaking the standoff. The Rebel position was certainly best disposed to receive an attack along the bridge itself, which was precisely the reason to avoid one. With the arrival of the Second Brigade under the peculiarly named Colonel Greenberry Wiles, Force took the path of least resistance by having his men attempt to wade across the swamp. Plunging into the swampy morass, Yankees sank up to their necks, discovering the stream was impassable. Wading the creek would certainly not do.

Force's command would have to risk concentrated Rebel fire and cross the intact bridge. Fortunately, he had enough manpower and the long arm of artillery to do just that. Giving the Rebels reason to give more thought to taking cover than fighting, Force unlimbered two guns of the Fifteenth Ohio Battery. The twin Yankee guns cranked into action, shelling the Confederate position. Darkness came, providing some natural stealth to mask the Yankees' movements. Under the covering fire of the artillery and sharpshooters, Force threw a column across the bridge. Realizing it was time to bail, the Rebels fled the scene, leaving some camp equipment and rations behind in the woods as spoils of war.

Force's victory did not clear up his situation. He still believed enemy forces were all around him. Irritatingly, the chieftain also found a discrepancy with his map. Local citizens claimed to have never heard of Angley's post office, although his map showed the location to be near. Cautiously, Force decided to throw a brigade on either side of the bridge and encamp for the night.

Force's wisdom was later confirmed when one of Howard's staff disclosed the object of his foray was to secure the bridge for the Fifteenth Corps just to the south. Another mystery was solved when an old African American man cleared up the confusion over Angley's post office. The name had been discontinued about three or four decades before, but Force was right where he needed to be. Leaving a regiment to guard the crossing, on February 3, Force moved toward Rivers' Bridge. There he rejoined the Seventeenth Corps in reserve while his comrades lay in mortal struggle just ahead.[116]

Chapter 7

Yanks, You Better Leave This Country

First blood had been drawn on the Salkehatchie. Confederates had stopped running, and finally the force of arms temporarily halted Sherman. Ironically, the Seventeenth Corps was suffering vicariously. Compared to the devastation wrought by the Twentieth and Fifteenth Corps, the men locked in a death struggle along the Salkehatchie had been angels. With three wrecked towns to their credit, Sherman's men would shortly meet more Confederates out to make them "leave this country."

While Blair moved on Rivers' Bridge on February 2, the Twentieth Corps moved north from Robertville to Lawtonville with Ward's division in the lead. Selfridge's brigade would be left behind to guard the landing and prepare the roads for the movement of the Fourteenth Corps. In effect, Williams was stepping off with all that existed of the Left Wing in South Carolina. After reaching Lawtonville, Williams would move on Duck Branch post office and close the gap between Sherman's two wings.[117]

Around 2:30 that afternoon, the boys of Colonel Henry Case's First Brigade probably felt an extra bounce in their step from freshly issued rations. Then, the crackle of musketry greeted their column three quarters of a mile from Lawtonville. The sounds were no mere potshots or men taking ill-advised shots at game. A brigade of about five hundred of Wheeler's cavalry had interrupted the column. Supported by two artillery pieces, the Rebels manned rail barricades just within the edge of a swamp outside town.[118] Protected by the swamp's natural cover, the Rebels had open field in their front, leaving the Federals caught well out in the open. In the words of one Yankee, they had "found Rebels."

Undaunted, Case quickly shook out the 105th Illinois as skirmishers on either side of the road to test the Rebel mettle. These Rebels held fast and matched the Yankees lead for lead. A nearby comrade of the 102nd Illinois recalled the scene vividly: "Sharp firing then commenced, the Rebels blazing away from behind trees and logs while many of the '105th' boys stood up in the road without protection, firing rapidly, round after round, at the concealed foe."[119] Caught in the open field, the 105th boys ground to a halt. Eight of their comrades lay either wounded in the field or slinking to the rear, having been struck by Rebel lead. It just so happened they had found Rebels with pluck.

More punch being needed, the big guns were brought forward. A section of Captain Charles E. Winegar's First New York Light Artillery, Battery M, unlimbered on a rise in the field about three or four hundred yards' distance and lined up their sights on the barricade. At least a dozen shells barked from Winegar's guns, sending rails flying from their bursts. Unfortunately for the stalled Federals, their adversaries showed no intentions of leaving so early. It would take more than a Yankee regiment and well-placed artillery rounds to run them off.

Feeding more irons in the fire, Case formed the 129th Illinois, 102nd Illinois and 70th Indiana on the flank of the bogged-down 105th Illinois. The skirmish line now extended to over a mile wide. As the line moved forward with a yell, the "galling" Rebel fire continued unabated into the surging blue wave. A man of the 102nd Illinois fell dead instantly, while two more comrades collapsed with wounds. One of the wounded lads joined his lifeless comrade shortly later.

Numbers and space got the better part of Southern valor. Now overlapping the Rebel line, Case swung his two wings around to outflank the defenders. For the Yanks preparing to advance on the works, a hard rush to remove the Rebels was seemingly moments away, but the flanking movement had its desired effect. As Yankees overran the barricades, the stubborn Rebels were found to have slinked away into the swamp. Its tangled morass had offered a natural screen for the troopers to evacuate the works.

If the Confederates expected any kind of respite, they were sadly mistaken. Case's skirmishers sharply drove the retreating defenders through Lawtonville, removing any further Confederate shenanigans. To be safe, the overly extended Federal pursuers fell back to their own lines after compelling Wheeler's troopers to "get up and travel."

Casualties had been sharp for both sides. Two Federals were dead and twelve wounded, with eight of the wounded being from the 105th Illinois, which had met such a sharp rebuff in the skirmish's early moments. The 102nd Illinois also had its share of casualties with two men killed and another wounded. The 129th Illinois itself had only one man wounded despite the Confederate fire that was, in the words of its commander, "pretty rapid." Ward reported his men killing eight and wounding thirty or forty Rebels. For Ward's division, Lawtonville was a far tougher prize to win than Hardeeville had been.

Though driven from the town, the Confederates could take some solace in the fact that they had given ground grudgingly. As they trotted off, they could at least quip among each other that it had taken what a Yankee participant would call a "Sherman battle in miniature" to dislodge them.[120] Interestingly enough, Yankee skirmishers found at least one explicit parting sign of defiance. A note left behind opined, "Yanks, you better leave this country, for France and England have recognized the Southern Confederacy, and Lincoln is ordered to withdraw his troops from our soil."[121]

While the Seventeenth Corps was conquering the Salkehatchie, the Fifteenth Corps had settled into a waiting game. As such, the corps spent February 3 in the area of Duck Creek. Rainfall made movement along the roads quite a difficult affair for Logan's command. However, the day would not be without those skirmishes that had already become a fixture. On February 3, the Forty-eighth Illinois outflanked a body of Rebels from their position across Duck Creek. One man was killed and another wounded in the small bit of fighting required.[122] The fighting was not merely an infantry affair, as the First Illinois Light Artillery, Company H, fired off five rounds to help dispatch the Confederates.

In another show of force, the Fourth Minnesota crossed Duck Creek in the face of a Rebel detachment. In a fight characteristic of the campaign thus far, the regiment was thrown forward with four companies of skirmishers and a strong reserve. Contested more by the three-foot-deep creek than Rebel lead, the Yankee skirmishers sent the Confederates to flight. The Yankees did amuse themselves handily as they discovered one of South Carolina's reptile residents concealed in the mud. The seven-foot alligator offered a few moments of excitement as it swung its huge tail toward its tormentors.[123] Ironically, Sherman's swamp-wading soldiers probably had more in common with this swamp dweller than their Confederate counterparts.

Fluid is the one word that best describes the movements of Sherman's columns by this time. Though now concentrating, they would soon spread out like dividing hydra. The day saw the arrival of Major General Williams's command at the Coosawhatchie Swamp not far from the Duck Branch post office, near the junction of the Orangeburg and Barnwell Roads. The ten-mile march through a drizzling rain was described as "delightful" by one of Williams's chipper troops. Sherman's patience had paid off. Just across the Coosawhatchie at Loper's Crossroads, the Fifteenth Corps awaited Williams's arrival. Elements of the Left Wing had now connected with the Right Wing. The entire army in South Carolina was now within a few dozen miles of each other and ready to move in concert.

Williams's arrival now gave Sherman the option of feinting to his west toward Barnwell and inevitably Augusta to baffle the Confederates. Avoiding the deep waters of the Coosawhatchie Swamp, Williams marched his command on February 4 via a settlement road through swampy environs to Smyrna Post Office. From Smyrna, Williams swung up Barnwell Road in the direction of Allendale.

Williams faced only poor roads as opposition on his eight-mile march to Smyrna Post Office. In fact, once Williams reached that point and turned his command north, he found the march far more favorable. Traveling through virgin territory, Williams found plenty of forage to feed his command. In one noted instance, Lieutenant Colonel Frederick C. Winkler recounts his forage party returning to camp with an "abundance of supplies" while others reined in sixteen horses and mules from the surrounding farms.[124] A couple of Yankees were more specific in bragging on their spoils. They recalled appetizing victuals like peanuts, sweet potatoes, chicken, molasses, butter and the ever-desired fresh pork abundant in the new country beyond Lawtonville.[125]

Good forage was not the only highlight of Williams's improved route. Beautiful country met Williams's column as it left Lawtonville. The ground seemed to "lift up" out of the swamps, and a cheerful demeanor drifted through Williams's column. A half mile beyond Lawtonville, a "palatial residence" awaited the Yankees. Until recently, this home of a Confederate officer had served as Wheeler's headquarters and was described this way by a Federal: "The grounds were ornamented in the finest style, with a rich variety of shrubbery. The house was magnificently furnished. The richest of carpets covered the floors; splendidly bound books ornamented the library; a sweet-toned piano was in the parlor."

Laconically, the same soldier reported the fate of the splendid home: "In accordance with orders received from a proper source, the building was burned." As if to dispel notions of this being an isolated case, our loyal correspondent from yesteryear noted "a number" of other similar dwellings burned according to orders.[126] Another Yankee soldier, incidentally a chaplain, waxed didactic when it came to the destruction. Echoing the words of his "flock," the man of God concluded that the "boys reasoned correctly" that since the wealthy of the South had led the country into secession, it was fit to "let them suffer—let South Carolina aristocracy have its fill of secession."[127] In coming days, the preacher took on Old Testament fervor, describing ruin and desolation everywhere one could turn. Columns of black smoke emerged over the trees in all directions, while buildings were left in flames, accompanied by chants of "Go it South Carolina," "South Carolina, the traitor's doom" and "How do you do, South Carolina?"

In at least one instance, the bonds of yesteryear overpowered desire for vengeance. At Woodstock Plantation near Lawtonville, Yankee torches never consumed the home. Fortunately, a Union officer's inquiry of the home's ownership identified Alfred Martin, a Confederate officer, as the owner. Recalling the happier times of Martin vacationing at resort town Saratoga Springs, New York, the officer spared the home.[128] Hardly unheard of, such reprieves do indicate at least some fondness for the happier times of antebellum bliss.

The times were not always pleasant, particularly for Federal wagons and their fraught guards. Wheeler's cavalry hovered along the column, threatening to take advantage of any opportunity to wipe out a foraging party or unprotected wagon team. In one notable case, a squad of Confederate cavalry killed three men of the Thirty-third Indiana. The price for wandering beyond their lines was steep indeed. Another complication was the poor roads. "Quicksands" crippled wagons, as wheels often sank up to their hubs.[129] It was certainly a mixed bag for Williams, but his column was moving right along.

Williams's movement screened another pivotal development. On February 3, Major General Judson Kilpatrick moved his five thousand troopers across the Savannah. This passing across the freshly built bridge and corduroyed roads meant that the rest of the army was finally able to cross into South Carolina. Kilpatrick's division would make up Sherman's cavalry contingent and consisted of three mounted and one dismounted brigade along with a six-gun battery.

Kilpatrick rode his command through the pitiful remnants of Robertville. The following day, Kilpatrick moved twelve miles to equally decimated Lawtonville.[130] When a curious Union soldier inquired the whereabouts of the town during one of its occupations, a local slave replied "you done be dar." The soldier then looked around to notice that scattered around the road were chimneys of a half dozen burned houses and a half-demolished church.[131] Like Robertville, Lawtonville does not exist as a town to this day.

Chapter 8

Build Them Strong, Catterson

The Seventeenth Corps had done well at Rivers' Bridge. The Salkehatchie had been forced in at least two locations. By day's end of February 4, two of its divisions had crossed and entrenched along the river with another division left to cross by day's end. For the Right Wing though, there still remained the Fifteenth Corps to cross. When and where this occurred would determine how quickly Sherman's army could move north. Without the same kind of dash exhibited by the Seventeenth Corps, the "whole army" may have to indeed cross at the solitary crossing at River's Bridge.

Early on February 4, the Fifteenth Corps resumed their march. As a precaution, Hazen's Second Division held tight to Angley's post office to block any Rebel threat from the direction of Barnwell. Woods's First Division took the lead with a light brigade (undelayed by wagons) thrown forward to secure the crossing of the Salkehatchie River at Buford's Bridge.[132]

Peculiarly, Buford's Bridge was not just a river crossing. There the bridge crossed the river's sixty-foot span, but its surrounding swamps stretched to over a mile wide. Eventually a village rose up on the northeast bank to serve weary travelers fresh across the swamp. Another stimulus was the village's proximity to the "crossroads" of the Barnwell Road with the road to Orangeburg. Both left their mark in the village's moniker. The village would assume the name of its nearby thoroughfare, Buford's Bridge. For old-timers, the more ancient name "the crossroads" seemed more fitting.

The earliest settlement in what is now Bamberg County, the village had several stores, a tailor shop, a shoe shop and a couple of grogshops. It was

The "dense jungle" bordering Buford's Bridge. *Courtesy of the author.*

the latter places of drunken revelries that helped stimulate the occasional brawl as men took off their coats and rolled up their sleeves to scrap in a ring outlined in the sand. These fights ended only when a beaten participant uttered, "Take him off!!" Equally drained travelers could break up their trip at the village boardinghouse.

For those of more dignified pursuits, a Masonic hall called the village home. Philadelphia Academy offered an intellectual stimulus for a "goodly" number of young people educated within its walls. Finally, Mispah Methodist Church served the village's spiritual needs. The relatively new structure was built in 1856 to replace its nearby predecessor. Buford's Bridge was a village like many others. But like the men who had brawled in its streets, the village now found itself in the ring with a devastating opponent.[133]

Its position on a main road led Major General McLaws to put a sizeable garrison at the village. Colonel Washington Hardy's North Carolina brigade manned an extensive line of earthworks blocking the bridge. Augmenting their numbers were the Eighth Texas and Fourth Tennessee Cavalry Regiments. Surely with their entrenched position there was enough manpower to contest a Yankee crossing. At the very least, McLaws's men

A city on a hilltop: Mispah Methodist Church. *Courtesy of the author.*

would sell it at a cost as dire as Rivers' Bridge downstream. Orders were given that the bridge was to be torched at the first sight of Yankees.

As battle raged at Rivers' Bridge, the garrison at Buford's Bridge assumed a Federal thrust stymied downstream would strike their lines next. With pickets extended across the river, the waiting game commenced. Around dark on February 3, a courier raced into the North Carolinians' lines. McLaws's lines had been broken was his dire report, and Hardy's men now found themselves cut off. Outflanked but not defeated, the North Carolinians had no choice but to retreat north toward the South Carolina Railroad at Lowry's Station (Bamberg).

A detachment of cavalry covering their rear, Hardy's men abandoned their works. The diminutive rear guard made use of the narrow roadways through the swamps to check any pursuit, but its young leader paid dearly with his life protecting the retreat. His tragic death and subsequent burial by the roadside marked the only evidence of any bloodshed in uprooting the strong Rebel bastion at Buford's Bridge.[134]

For Logan's vanguard, the march to Buford's Bridge had little drama. Predictably, when Woods's division arrived, they found twenty-six bridges through the milelong swamp wrecked. Rebels had also partially destroyed the bridge.[135] But ahead lay a sight that instilled chills down Woods's spine—the abandoned Confederate entrenchments. That a battle here could have inflicted quite a severe loss on Logan's corps seemed a consensus by many of the Union witnesses. Major George Nichols of Sherman's staff recounted the abandoned fortification with an obvious sense of relief. It is worth quoting in its entirety:

> *Today I have examined the works at Beaufort Bridge, which were evacuated by the Rebels as soon as we made the crossing at Rivers' Bridge. The place is remarkably strong, both in its natural advantages and in the line of works which defend the passage. A brigade, with a single section of artillery, could have held an army at bay. So it would seem, at least, when one wades and stumbles over the narrow road which leads for half a mile through the swamp. Emerging from the dense jungle before crossing the main branch of the stream, one may see upon its border a line of well-built works extending for a quarter of a mile on either side. Here are three embrasures, pierced for heavy guns, while the parapet is surmounted by the protecting head-log. If the enemy had not been flanked below, and could have defended this place, its capture would have cost us hundreds of lives.*

Nichols's description provides us the image of a fight that could have been as costly as Rivers' Bridge. Major General Woods, whose division went to work repairing the wrecked causeway, was best suited to give impressions on the ground. Looking at the swamps occupying his men, Woods opined that the position could not be carried by an assault because of its "natural obstacles." Our witness to this flattering quip, Major Henry Hitchcock, gives an even better picture of the swampy morass:

> *It is nearly or quite a mile across the river and swamp, the river proper being on the farther or northern side. The road is narrow, hardly wide enough for two wagons to pass; the ground always soft and muddy, the impenetrable trees and bushes on both sides standing in water and mud, all along, the road itself being a dirt causeway thrown up. Every little while, there was a "bridge," or rather a sort of wooden culvert, twenty-seven in all, to allow passage to the sluggish current…The road was more or less winding through the swamp, and the water grew deeper as we approached the other bank, and in some places flowed over the hasty bridges or "corduroys."*

Nichols recounted the sounds of axes and cries of the pioneers as they hacked away. Half-burned stringers were used whenever possible, while timbers taken from a local church or downed trees made up the slack. On top of these were laid planking "corduroy style" supplied by more swamp timber, fence rails or planking from existing buildings.[136] This makeshift bridging would have to bear the weight of tramping feet, stamping horses and lumbering wagons through a mile of swamp.

Although less than ideal, the rough corduroy would have to do. While supervising the work, Colonel Robert F. Catterson, commander of the Second Brigade, was admonished by no less a figure than Sherman himself. "Build them strong Catterson, build them strong; the whole army may have to pass over them and the Army of the Cumberland is a very heavy army, sir."[137] Slight jesting aside, the anecdote is a striking reminder of how fluid the situation was for Sherman's embryonic invasion. The hard work paid off, and apparently the bridges were built plenty strong. By the following day, Logan had pushed his corps across the morass and taken positions around town.

There would be no measure of defense for the town itself, as the hamlet would not survive Federal occupation. Unlike the fisticuff matches that once

Where "quite the little settlement" of Buford's Bridge once stood. *Courtesy of the author.*

marked its streets, there was no heeding the call to "take him off." With the exception of the Mispah Methodist Church, Buford's Bridge would be destroyed off the map. One of Woods's soldiers recalled the village of twenty to twenty-five homes "used up" in constructing bridges.[138] Interestingly, our previous diarist Hitchcock noted, "There was quite a little settlement, not quite a village" where Buford's Bridge once lay.[139] His choice of the past tense is revealing. To this day, only a short, stone marker (which strikingly resembles a tombstone) and a metallic historical marker offer an epitaphic reminder of the destroyed village that once thrived at Buford's Bridge.

Chapter 9

Those Fellows Are Trying to Stop Us

Crossing the Salkehatchie River had been a costly affair. Over one hundred Federals lay either in "hospitable graves" or were en route to hospitals at Beaufort. Now there was a chance that Confederates with more spunk, and maybe a bit of sass, waited eagerly at the Little Salkehatchie. In search of what lay ahead, Logan sent fifty mounted men to that river on February 5. The open country beyond gave extra wiggle room to make blockading pointless, allowing Logan's scouts to work to the river with little trouble.

There the detachment found the road through the three-hundred-foot swamp obstructed as usual and the bridge burned. Logan's scouts did learn that a brigade of the enemy allegedly held the opposite bank, and the area through which he was to march would be filled with plenty of good forage. Another party scouted the roads leading from Rivers' Bridge, finding much the same. In fact, the information learned by these forays convinced Howard to wait until the following day to force the Little Salkehatchie. While withdrawing, the Yankees left word with locals that they would be back with more friends. Another fight was brewing, and this time it could likely involve the entire Right Wing.

With the abandonment of the Salkehatchie, Wheeler moved his cavalry to cover the Little Salkehatchie. The road from Buford's Bridge crossed the river at Lane's Bridge while the road from Rivers' and Broxton's Bridges combined to cross the same stream at Cowpen Ford. Brigadier General William Allen took up covering the approach up the Buford Bridge Road with his division while Brigadier General William Humes's division covered the road from Rivers' Bridge.

One of numerous streams at Cowpen Ford on the Little Salkehatchie. *Courtesy of the author.*

Wheeler did not have long to wait, as the Yankees returned as promised with company. At 7:00 a.m., his pickets were once again forced into action.[140] Somewhere in the rear were the two columns of the Seventeenth Corps moving via the two roads from the Salkehatchie River. Blair had ordered Force's Third Division to swing up the Broxton's Bridge and Midway Road. Directly following Force was Mower's First Division, while the Ninth Illinois Mounted Infantry led the right-hand column's advance. Bifurcating the column into two wings, Smith's Fourth Division traveled straight up the Rivers' Bridge and Midway Road. Both wings would converge at Cowpen Ford.

Made up of the Twentieth Illinois and other mounted detachments, the Yankee vanguard pitched into Confederates at the ford. Strung out in rifle pits across the river was a brigade of about six hundred of Humes's cavalry ready to offer another stout stand. Aiding in their defense, the river consisted of a daunting nine streams. The Southern troopers stood poised to make sure crossing each and every one of them would be costly.

Force's advance pushed through a half a mile of the morass bordering the river. With one detachment skirmishing directly up the road, more Yankees searched for the Rebel flank. Battling the head of a Yankee corps, the Rebel troopers kept up a game fight for an hour and a half before being outflanked and forced to retreat.[141] But according to one adversary, they had "fought well."[142] Behind them lay empty air where the burned bridges once lay. Confidently, Howard sent word to Sherman that he should have the seven bridges across the river repaired in only two hours.

Howard's confidence was misplaced. A closer inspection revealed that the bridges had been thoroughly destroyed. Every stringer had either been burned or cut into. Howard would have to spend five hours repairing the 262 feet of bridging across the river.[143] The thorough destruction of the bridges proved that the greatest enemy challenging Sherman's army was not Confederate rifles but the smoking ruins of destroyed bridges. A day that had begun with so much promise had broken down into hours of tedious labor. Consequently, only Force's division got across the river that day.

The same morning, the Fifteenth Corps advanced on Lane's Bridge, twelve miles north on the Buford's Bridge Road. Smith's Third Division had the lead with the mounted men of the Twenty-ninth Missouri Mounted Infantry out front. Smith, the son of an immigrant who had once fought on the field of Waterloo, certainly could not expect the grandeur of Napoleonic fighting on this day.[144] At the very least, Smith could hope that his trip would be smoother than his earlier days tramping through overflowed South Carolina rice fields and submerged wells.

The Yankees met Rebel pickets and found just what was expected.[145] There the Federals found the defense they had become accustomed to, as falling timber obstructed the causeway. A thick, tangled swamp stretched several miles below the position, while opening into a pond above the crossing. The Yankees did hold a high bluff, but beyond lay a seemingly impassable swamp that supposedly held a brigade of Confederates. Seeing another example of the "miserable" Palmetto swamp barriers, one Federal witness seemed unsurprised. The scene of "water not often deep—woods and thickets dense on both sides, sometimes almost absolutely impassable for a single footman, sometimes not so" had certainly been seen before.[146]

Looking for a less-guarded crossing, the mounted Twenty-ninth Missouri was sent three or four miles below the bridge to a good candidate while the Seventh Illinois scoured the riverbank for one of their own. At the bridge, skirmishers probed through the knee-deep swamp to learn what force lay concealed on the northern bank. Their answer was quite a bit and that it stretched awfully far. A brigade of 1,200 to 1,500 of Allen's troopers was found entrenched in a strong line of rifle pits extending quite some distance below and above the bridge.

Another "miserable" stretch of the Little Salkehatchie. *Courtesy of the author.*

Surveying the scene, corps commander Logan found that this time there would be a fight for Smith's hard-luck division. Into the fray, Smith committed Wever's Second Brigade. The Tenth Iowa swung off three-quarters of a mile to the left of the road and the Eightieth Ohio about the same distance to the right to shore up the flanks. These two flanking regiments were authorized to force a crossing if possible and turn the Confederates' flanks. In the center overlapping the road was the Fifty-sixth Illinois. In their hands would lay the direct assault into the teeth of the Confederate defenses.

All signs pointed to a stubborn defense. As Logan surveyed the pandemonium, his irritation with the enemy showed. "Those fellows are trying to stop us at the creek down there, and d— sassy they are acting about it," exclaimed the miffed politician general.[147] Daring the defenders to disclose any artillery, a section of the First Michigan Light Artillery, Company B's three-inch Rodman guns rolled into action. After six shells without retaliation, Smith was confident enough to order the Fifty-sixth Illinois forward.

The Illinoisans plunged into the waist-deep river. Confederates opened with sharp fire while game Yankees waded through the muck. As if egged on by the rattle of musketry, Wever's boys would not be denied as they forced their way through, fighting swamp, river and piercing lead. Daunted, the Rebels found themselves fighting amphibians rather than men. With the Yankee momentum threatening to run right over their parapets and into their laps, the Rebels abandoned their works.

With a lot of pluck and raw audacity, Wever had dispatched a Rebel force of comparable numbers. Recollecting their senses, the uprooted Confederates rallied on a ridge about a half a mile from the river before being forced back toward Graham's Turnout and the railroad. With the cost of five wounded, the Fifteenth Corps had crossed the Little Salkehatchie after a three-hour fight. Its bridge was repaired, and the entire corps moved over the river during the afternoon and night hours.[148]

Logan went into camp at Springtown Meeting House while Smith and Sherman occupied the two-and-a-half-story home of Dr. Fishburne. Other officers shared somewhat with the men as they pitched tent flies under the stars in a severe rain. For Hitchcock, the dripping rain from an overhanging tree annoyed an otherwise sound, dry sleep.[149] For those less fortunate, Wever's brigade probably looked on with amusement at the prospect of a wet night for their comrades who had been spared their turn wading the swamps.

Chapter 10

Nothing in South Carolina Was Held Sacred

It is ironic that South Carolina, firstborn among the Confederacy, was one of the last to have Northern invaders step foot on its interior. In the midst of another sectional squabble over nullification, the state's governor looked hypothetically to a day when the state's "sacred soil" would be "polluted" by an invader's boots.[150] Little would he know that just over three decades later, an invader would treat nothing in South Carolina sacred.

While Howard drove Wheeler's troopers from the Little Salkehatchie, Williams's Twentieth Corps was in movement. On February 5, Williams moved by way of Buford's Bridge before coming via a parallel road to rest near Logan's newly won position at the Little Salkehatchie. It had been a twenty-five-mile march over two days; nevertheless, the Twentieth Corps now sat only a day's march from striking the Charleston–Augusta Railroad to their north.[151]

Williams's march was both prosperous and punitive. Forage was plentiful, as fowl, swine and fruits of the earth abounded "amid rejoicings" by hungry soldiers.[152] The abundance was the product of a special brand of boldness, as foragers ranged widely. Other less scrupulous plunderers ranged independently, not fearing God, man nor his "mythical majesty, the devil." Once again, the "valiant, last ditch" chivalry's suffering was evident, as all around pillars of dark smoke rose.[153] Plantations fueled the pillars, and even white flags were just a "trifle late." Those with sympathy to the Union were not immune, as raiders set fire to a Lincoln man's barn before more sensible minds arrived to extinguish it.[154] According to one Yankee's recollections, the festivities meant, "South Carolina's punishment had begun."[155]

If a Union soldier's words are to be trusted, punishment wasn't only inflicted by Federals. As Yankees rampaged throughout the countryside, citizens cried foul at abuses. "You are unfortunate living in this state, for South Carolina is bound to suffer" was one of the Northerners' replies. Curiously, the citizen responded that this was just the way Wheeler's cavalry talked as they came to homes, demanding citizens shell out their stuff since they "commenced this muss."[156]

Meanwhile, Kilpatrick's cavalry was continuing toward Barnwell. To Sherman, Barnwell's importance was minimal, as he merely saw it as a place to cross the Salkehatchie River and swamps at nearby Morris Ford. From Barnwell, Kilpatrick would strike the railroad somewhere between Blackville and Lowry's Station.[157] Combined with the remaining three corps, this would put Sherman striking the railroad in four places on February 7. The arrangement would send chills up Confederate spines. There were scarcely enough men to make a stand at one point along the railroad, much less four.

On February 5, Kilpatrick's command moved toward Allendale, "burning and destroying everything" as they went. It was near this hamlet that Kilpatrick chose Roselawn, the home of Minister Joseph Lawton, as his headquarters. The preacher's family found themselves exiled to a small room to make way for their new squatters.[158] Remedying their inconvenience, at least their home was spared the torch. Kilpatrick afterward turned his column toward Barnwell and Morris Ford.[159]

The Ninth Ohio Cavalry of Brigadier General Smith D. Atkins's Second Brigade was the first to find Confederate resistance at the crossing. These buckeyes under Colonel William D. Hamilton found a small regiment of Confederate troopers well entrenched on the elevated opposite bank. The bridge had been lit ablaze by the defenders, and the thick swamp offered a stout challenge to cross. To get things rolling, a couple of companies headed into the waist-deep water as skirmishers to find the Rebel left flank.

Meanwhile, Kilpatrick unlimbered Lieutenant Oscar A. Clark's Tenth Wisconsin Artillery Battery and put them to work. Filling out the line to the left, the Ninety-second Illinois Mounted Infantry under Lieutenant Colonel Matthew Van Buskirk were dismounted and thrown forward with their Spencer carbines to ford the swamp along the Confederate right. Buskirk's men waded through armpit-deep water and crossed fallen logs to cross the river. Rising out of the morass, Buskirk's men set their sights on the Rebels.

With both flanks turned, Yankee shells falling and Bushkirk's warriors charging their earthworks, the disheartened Confederates lost their will. The troopers abandoned their earthworks and fled the scene in confusion. Their retreat left behind one dead and three men wounded. They also left Barnwell totally at the mercy of Kilpatrick's troopers. For the town's citizens, the unthinkable had arrived as hooves clopped along the partially destroyed bridge.

If the citizens of Barnwell expected a mild hand, they would be sadly mistaken. For some, the skirmishing had moved to their very doorsteps. Just outside of town, Mrs. Alfred Proctor Aldrich heard the boom of Kilpatrick's artillery at Morris Ford as a "death-knell." Another lady, Sarah Jane Graham Sams, nearly found herself a casualty as Kilpatrick's troopers took a last dig at tardy Rebels in town. Though balls flew, she was thankfully unhurt as she watched the last-minute skirmishing from her piazza.

Mrs. Aldrich perhaps captured the heartfelt emotions of many neighbors as the first "blue coats" raced up the road toward her home. Their protectors had now withdrawn "wrapped in overcoats or gray blankets, with bent heads before the chilling rain."[160] Looking at the first of many of Kilpatrick's troopers to rampage through her town, Aldrich recalled the "horrible accounts we had for months been listening to of the brutal treatment of the army to the women of Georgia." Subsequent events would make her fears well founded. At the Aldrich home and others throughout Barnwell, the terror began:

> They were pouring in every door, and without asking to have bureaus and wardrobes opened, broke with their bayonets every lock, tearing out the contents, in hunting for gold, silver, and jewels, all of which had been sent off weeks before. Finding nothing to satisfy their cupidity so far, they began turning over mattresses, tearing open feather-beds, and scattering the contents in the wildest confusion.

The discovery of unfortunately unhidden whiskey pushed the destruction beyond mere plunder:

> Tables were knocked over, lamps with their contents thrown over carpets and mattings, furniture of all sorts broken, a guitar and violin smashed. The piano escaped in the general wreck—why I could never understand. Provisions as much as they wanted were carried off. The policy of first comers seemed to be not to ruin or destroy any food, but to leave all they did not require for those that were to come after.

Soon, Mrs. Sams found her home besieged by Kilpatrick's marauders. Perhaps curious of their growing reputation, a Yankee rhetorically asked

Sherman's cavalier: Brigadier General Judson Kilpatrick. *Courtesy of the Library of Congress.*

Sams about the treatment she expected. Speaking a refrain straight from the chivalry catechism, she replied that she always expected civil and polite treatment from gentlemen. Amused, the Yankee poked fun at the very rumors of improprieties that begat his question. In a remark sure to be believed, he quipped, "There are no gentlemen in the Union army, we are all convicts turned out to end the Rebellion." Unnerved, Mrs. Sams's "ma" insisted that surely the officers would treat them as ladies. The Union soldier confidently quipped, "You will find the officers worse than the men." A few days later this statement would be eerily prophetic as a new batch of Yankees entered town.

Mrs. Sams would grow to trust that the Yankee trooper's dissertation was not far off base. As she watched Kilpatrick's troopers kick down fences, smash their way into doors, shatter glasses and tear up clothing, the Union soldiers appeared to her less human than beasts. The "convicts" behaved more like "enraged tigers than human beings." Throughout town fires broke out in offices, stable buildings and homes, leaving some citizens forced to the streets. One unfortunate individual had his store fired twice, only to have the flames extinguished. Unfortunately, as Mrs. Aldrich would opine, "nothing in South Carolina was held sacred." Her husband's office and the seemingly untouchable Masonic Hall were both fired, which emblazoned the store once again.[161]

Mrs. Aldrich's consternation over the Masonic Hall's fate is understood considering a curious event in the early minutes of the ordeal. As he came into town, Colonel Hamilton found himself approached by a party of Masons' wives who used the ancient order's bond of brotherhood to solicit protection. Hamilton denied any Masonic affiliation and avowed that none of his command would use the esteemed order to avoid his sworn duty. The burning of the Masonic Hall, along with the "archives, jewels, and sacred emblems of the order so reverenced by Masons everywhere," confirmed his stoic pronouncement.[162] Coincidentally, Hamilton did assure the delegation that his men were gentlemen who would treat them as ladies. Whether the "convict" element about town heard and enjoyed his unintended irony went unrecorded.

When all was said and done, Kilpatrick laid much of the town to the torch. All of the public buildings were burned as well as a number of private homes. In one of the least charming moments of a less-than-charming career, Kilpatrick suggested to Sherman that he should rename the town "Burnwell" following his stay.[163] Kilpatrick's pun alone gives credence that some Yankee officers were, in fact, worse than their men.

The following day, Wheeler set out from Graham's Turnout for the railroad town of Blackville. There he had about one hundred men from Hagan's Alabama brigade (Allen's division) posted as pickets. Hagan's men should have seen it coming. Perhaps they did. Regardless, on the morning of February 7, Kilpatrick's column arrived at Blackville. Colonel Thomas Jordan's First Brigade led the column as its lead regiment, the Third Kentucky Cavalry, smashed into Hagan's pickets and occupied the town.

Overwhelmed, Hagan's men retired while the Second Kentucky Cavalry and a company of the Ninth Pennsylvania Cavalry pursued closely. The chase was on for three miles as Jordan's troopers snatched up stray Rebels and mounts in the precipitous retreat.

Salvation was ahead as Brigadier General George Dibrell's cavalry brigade wheeled into line to stem the tide. The pursuing Yankees now found a brigade of Rebels blocking their pursuit. Dibrell's men shortly began turning the Yankees' flank. Realizing discretion is the better part of valor, the pursuers broke contact to retreat back to their own lines. Kilpatrick consolidated his forces at Blackville and went to work destroying the railroad. The short fight for Blackville was over. Fourteen Rebels had been captured and "a large number killed and wounded." Confederate losses were more definite in material. Kilpatrick's troopers destroyed a couple of miles of track, ten flat cars, the station house, seventy-five barrels of molasses and ninety boxes of tobacco.[164] Kilpatrick's men would shortly have company along the railroad.[165]

Chapter 11

A Hasty Visit to Mr. Simms

Wheeler's troopers had help on the way as remnants of the Army of Tennessee arrived. After the crushing defeat at Nashville in December 1864, the once proud army was in ruins. Although all three corps eventually were to arrive and help in the Carolinas, only Stephen D. Lee's corps was likely to arrive in time to fight south of Columbia. On January 29, a part of Lee's corps arrived via train in Augusta, Georgia. By February 3, Lee's corps was en route to Branchville, South Carolina, to take part in its defense.[166] Leading the corps was forty-seven-year-old Major General Carter Littlepage Stevenson. The Fredericksburg, Virginia native was a West Point graduate and had served in the U.S. Army in the Mexican War and on the frontier. Eventually he would be dismissed in June 1861 for having "entertained and expressed treasonable designs against the Government of the United States" after a mishandled resignation.

Now Stevenson found himself managing a "corps" of a little over two thousand men that lay directly in Sherman's path. It was quite an interesting turn for a man who less than two years earlier had surrendered at Vicksburg.[167] After his defeat on the Salkehatchie, McLaws marched his two-thousand-man division to Branchville to take positions along the Edisto River. To his west, Stevenson stretched his seven brigades along the South Edisto River.[168] Buying them time were Wheeler's troopers desperately trying to delay Sherman along the Little Salkehatchie.

At this time, we should familiarize ourselves with the Edisto River and its two tributaries. The Edisto and its northern and southern forks form what resembles a wishbone turned clockwise before turning roughly south to the coast. From the west, the south branch runs just north of the Charleston–Augusta Railroad while the north branch approaches Orangeburg from the west before heading south to strike the confluence of the three rivers just west of Branchville.

With Stevenson and McLaws entrenching, the stage for the coming fight was set. However, Sherman's officers still could only speculate as to what defense waited at the railroad. One Yankee witness called enemy dispositions a mystery, while citizens floated rumors that ranged from an extreme of Lieutenant General James Longstreet waiting ahead with fifteen thousand men to no opposition at all. All seemed to curse Confederate president Jefferson Davis for his lack of action. One piece of evidence promised more of the same. Passing Confederates left word with locals that they intended to make a severe fight along Lemon Swamp, just south of the railroad.[169]

On February 7, the Right Wing stepped off for the railroad. Ahead lay Lemon Swamp and a potentially "severe fight." Confederates left the usual fallen timber in the roads and burned bridges. The defenders, however, were

Lemon Swamp was the location of a "severe" fight that never came. *Courtesy of the author.*

strangely missing. So far, the only resistance was inclement rain that kept the water high and turned the roads into mush. The Fifteenth Corps made the five-mile march to the railroad quickly as two and a half hours after setting out, the Seventh Illinois and the Twenty-ninth Missouri Mounted Infantry seized Lowry's Station. By noon, Yankees were at work destroying the railroad. In fact, Logan's move was so rapid that he had two divisions entrenched covering approaches north of town by nightfall. The remaining division stayed south of the railroad guarding the wagon train from any bold move by Rebel horsemen.[170]

Though Wheeler's pickets had abandoned the town, there were visible reminders of their hasty withdrawal. About three hundred bales of cotton were left behind at the little railroad hamlet. Also abandoned was a peek into the Rebel psyche. A captured mailbag revealed letters written by demoralized Confederates in a "most desponding tone."[171] Local citizens sounded an equally defeatist tune as talk of peace and reconstruction was in the air.[172] Naturally the abandoned cotton was burned while the captured letters inflamed Yankee hearts as proof that the Confederacy's rank and file were on their last legs.

The Seventeenth Corps's move was more sluggish. Delayed by wretched roads and barricades, Blair's men rebuilt the three burned bridges at Lemon's Swamp. There was no "severe fight" to be had. Although a Rebel observation post held the swamp the day before, Logan's movements had removed any reason for sticking around. Once his column had crossed, Blair moved for the rail station at Midway to the north.[173]

Anxious over the prospect of a fight, Right Wing commander Howard watched the roads to the railroad, looking for a sign. Anxiety rose as he saw a lone rider hastily riding his way. The rider was mounted on a "good horse…with a rope bridle, rope stirrups, and an old blanket for a saddle." The rider's motley appearance could mean only one thing—a "bummer." Best described as empowered thieves masquerading as military foragers, even some of their own officers recognized their "foraging" for what it truly was. One Yankee officer damningly referred to their craft as "scientific and authorized stealing."[174] With a bummer racing into view, Howard must have wondered if one of the parties had run into far more than it could handle ahead. Such a development could portend a fight for the railroad. Perhaps the Confederates had a severe fight planned after all.

The bummer very excitedly informed Howard that he and a half a dozen of his comrades had seized the railroad at Midway. Shockingly, the messenger proclaimed that the squad of raiders was at that very moment holding off a riled-up detachment of Rebels. The idea that a few bummers had seized and now held the vital railroad was quite ludicrous to Howard. In light of the hilarity of the situation, Howard saw an opportunity to make sport of it all. An awkward specimen of soldier, the bummer was nonetheless sent reporting the same news to various other officers. All humor aside, a great relief had to swell over the Federals closing on the railroad. Sure enough, bummers "had" the railroad and were in a long-distance sparring contest with Rebels to see just how long they were willing to keep it. The arrival of Federal infantry convinced the Rebel party to give up their efforts. Thanks to the infamous bummers, Blair's Seventeenth Corps had seized the railroad.

The queerly named Midway owed its moniker to being the halfway point on the Charleston–Augusta (technically Hamburg) Railroad between the two cities. Like Lowry's Station a few miles to the west, cotton was left as booty. With a host of angry Yankees flooding the area, an unfortunate store owner pleaded for the safety of his two hundred bales of cotton on the clever grounds that he needed it to pay some "beeples" in New York to whom he owed some "little debts." Judging by events elsewhere, it isn't a leap to assume his pleading fell upon deaf ears, as our Yankee witness confidently proclaimed that he would "hardly save the cotton."[175]

Nearby was a site well worth saving for both intrinsic and extrinsic value. Woodlands, the plantation of famed nineteenth-century author William Gilmore Simms, sat quietly a few miles away. The grounds of the plantation had a personal library reputed to have had ten thousand volumes. One Yankee admiringly called it "one of the most valuable libraries we had met with in the seven Southern States which we had traversed."[176] Many of the books were gifts from the rich, the famous and the distinguished from both Europe and America—i.e. irreplaceable. With Sherman's army en route, Simms fled northwest to Columbia, leaving an "ardent secesh family" behind to watch over his plantation. Although the gorgeous original Simms mansion had been destroyed in a fire almost three years previously, the home had been rebuilt on a much smaller scale by early 1865.

Damningly for Simms, one Union soldier described Woodland's owner as a "prolific political writer and fiercest of voluble fire eaters."[177] Another officer described "Mr. Simms" as "a thorough, rabid secessionist, full of southern prejudices, and a fierce calumniator of northern character and institutions."[178] This made him certainly qualify as the chivalry and opened up his property to all that it would imply. Other accounts give snippets of sinister developments. Major Thomas Ward Osborn predicted that the "fine

The gate for Woodlands Plantation still stands prominently. *Courtesy of the author.*

library" at Woodlands would be saved but, in a chilling admission, said, "but I should have no objection to seeing it burned." It is worthy to note that another officer noted many books from Simms's library, marked with his very autograph, appearing in the Federal camp as "mementos."[179]

Hinting of Yankee mischief, one correspondent described the tumult when he boasted that "our skirmishers and foragers paid a hasty visit to Mr. Simms, and, as he was not at home, they thought they would do the honors of the house themselves, and fell to helping themselves liberally." Although guards were posted, they could not watch the home forever. Whatever occurred, Woodlands and its extensive library met the same fate as so many others and were likely decimated by Sherman's stragglers. The postwar incarnation of Woodlands is still held by the family that has admirably made great strides toward staying in contact with the descendants of the plantation's former slaves as part of their shared history.[180]

Ironically, this time was one of the more important steps of Sherman's campaign, as he had cited breaking up South Carolina's railroad system as one of his major goals. Sherman understood how this logistical coup would drive the final nail in the coffin of the doomed Confederacy. In the words of

Major George Ward Nichols, "Every tie burned and every rail twisted is an irretrievable damage to the Rebels."[181]

Sherman's operations around the railroad would not be pass and go. Sherman intended to wait on Major General Jefferson C. Davis's Fourteenth Corps to close the gap between themselves and the rest of the army before passing the South Edisto River. This delay would give the opportunity to destroy the railroad thoroughly. Looking ahead, Sherman began to show doubts about the flooded landscape in his path. Heavy rains and flooded creeks delayed him as much as Rebels, and Sherman conceded in a letter to Admiral Dahlgren commanding blockading forces off the coast that the swollen waters may force him to turn on Charleston yet.

As the Seventeenth Corps slowly overcame atrocious roads at Midway, skirmishing continued. Major General Blair took the liberty of sending a company of the Ninth Illinois Mounted Infantry in a reconnaissance to the aptly named Cannon's Bridge over the South Edisto. Predictably, there they found Rebel pickets on the south bank of the engorged river. The Yankee horsemen easily dispatched the outliers across the river, forcing them to torch two of the bridges behind them. Their goal accomplished, the Federal horsemen trotted back to camp.[182]

Of particular importance were two nearby Edisto River crossings. The railroad crossed the Edisto River east of the confluence. Sherman ordered Blair to remove that trestle bridge to protect his right flank from harassment. The Eleventh Iowa under Lieutenant Colonel Benjamin Beach drew the call to either force the Rebels to burn the bridge or destroy it themselves. The Confederates guarding the bridge found an angry adversary. The Iowans had marched fourteen miles that cold, rainy day and had just stacked arms to bivouac when orders came to fall in. Fortunately for their weary bodies, the bridge's defenders were in no mood to make the day any more troubling. As the Yankees approached, Rebel pickets heard them in the darkness. The Confederates exchanged a few shots and bailed across the bridge.[183] Much to the pleasure of the Yankees, the Rebels saved them the trouble by firing the bridge themselves. By midnight, Beach's exhausted command was back in camp; it had been a long day.

The other crossing was Walker's or Valley Bridge, the direct crossing of the Edisto into Branchville. On February 8, the Ninth Illinois Mounted Infantry was ordered out again, this time under Captain Henley of Blair's staff. Like most of the Edisto riverbanks, a tangled swamp bordered the river while a single causeway cut through the morass. Amid the formidable Edisto

A site of two skirmishes: the South Edisto River at Cannon's Bridge. *Courtesy of the author.*

swamps, Henley's troopers struck Rebel pickets south of the river and drove them back to the crossing.

Driven to the bridgehead, the pickets blocked a rush on the bridge. Henley's men kept up the pressure and soon dislodged the holdouts. The Rebels fell back across the incendiary-prepared bridge. In their wake, the bridge burst into flames. The customary defense was found, as a couple of regiments manned fortifications across the river. A section of artillery supported the Confederate riflemen and opened up in kind on Henley's checked troopers. With the bridge crackling in flames, Henley did not take the bait. The captain about-faced his detachment and trotted back to camp.[184]

Success notwithstanding, the feints were not over. Sherman wanted another look at Cannon's Bridge. Major General Hazen of the Fifteenth Corps was tasked to send a brigade to do just that. He dispatched Colonel Wells Jones's Second Brigade with a day's ration and full cartridge boxes in a reconnaissance to Cannon's Bridge to see what he could find out. Helping matters, the corps engineer officer accompanied the foray, lending his trained eye to the festivities.

What Jones faced was a five-mile march across flooded roads. In fact, Jones estimated a quarter of his route lay submerged. Closing on the river, a six-hundred-yard-wide swamp was found stretched along either side of the road. Jones threw forward four companies of the Fifty-fourth Ohio to push through. The Yankee skirmishers battled thigh- and waist-deep water as they sparred with the Rebels. Approaching to within a few rods of the burned bridge, they found a line of occupied Confederate works several hundred yards long across the river. Learning all he needed to know, Jones broke contact and marched back to camp with no casualties.[185]

With the railroad held in force from its bridge over the Edisto to Lowry's Station, the gap of unmolested railroad from Graham's Turnout to Blackville still remained to be neutralized. It was a gap that the Twentieth Corps waited to fill. We will recall that we last left the corps at Springtown Meeting House on the Little Salkehatchie. Williams's destination was Graham's Turnout on the railroad approximately ten miles southwest of Lowry's. On February 7, Williams pushed his command, with considerable difficulty, across the rain-swollen Little Salkehatchie. Rain began to pour as the strung-out column moved along a parallel road toward Graham's Turnout. Difficulties or not, advance regiments struck the railroad that afternoon a mile and a half east of Graham's at the fifty-mile post from Augusta, completing the nine-mile march.

While the corps consolidated, the men of the 107th New York moved on Graham's Turnout. Perhaps recalling earlier shenanigans, their orders were to guard personal and private property until the arrival of the main columns. The New Yorkers arrived around 7:00, found the town abandoned and established guards. With his forces now stretched for over fifteen miles along the railroad, Sherman began the track's destruction. Rails were to be removed, as well as heated, bent and twisted.[186] The systematic destruction was remembered in vivid detail by Sergeant Theodore F. Upson, who was not a stranger to the work:

> *The way this is done is to string the troops out along the track, two men to a tie. The men stick their guns with their bayonets on into the ground close behind them so as to have them handy in case of an attack, and then at a "yo heave!" evry man grabs a tie and lifts. Up comes the whole track and slowly tips over. Then with sledge hammers, hand spikes, or any thing else handy, the ties are knocked loose from the rails, the fish plates unbolted, the pine ties made into piles, set on fire, and the rails laid on top. When they get red hot in the center about 20 men get hold of the ends and wind them edgewise around a telegraph pole or small tree. That fixes them.[187]*

Sherman's men wrecking a line of track. *Courtesy of the Library of Congress.*

Seeking to "fix" the rail lines, the path of destruction began on February 8 near the railroad bridge and extended to west of Graham's Station. The only hint of resistance emerged at Graham's as an officer was approached by a lady with a sealed envelope left behind by Wheeler. It seemed a desperate attempt to prevent further destruction of civilian property. Wheeler attempted to arrange a quid pro quo with the Federals. If Sherman's men would cease burning homes, he would refrain from burning abandoned cotton. The white gold would be left in Federal hands to presumably be sold on the market. It amounted to a virtual payoff for Sherman's men to end their collateral destruction.

Unfortunately for South Carolinians, Sherman wanted no part. Sherman feigned no ambiguity when he ordered Williams to burn all cotton, rightly seeing it as the only cash left for the Confederacy. A personal response to Wheeler was just as resolute: "I hope you will burn all cotton and save us the trouble." Referring to it as that "curse to our country," Sherman vowed to burn any remaining cotton. Regarding the burning of homes, as noted earlier Sherman waxed plausible deniability, insisting that he "thought" his orders against molesting peaceful occupied homes were being obeyed. As for unoccupied dwellings, Sherman admitted he did not "take too much care to preserve them." The daily smoke trails on the horizon were proof of the sincerity in that statement.[188]

The "cursed" cotton did serve at least one good purpose before over 370 bales were resigned to the flames. A man of the Thirty-third Massachusetts noted with amusement the new "sensation" of laying upon $200 worth of captured cotton for a bed.[189] Other new sensations were found along the railroad. A chaplain with the Eighty-fifth Indiana sounded more the carnival barker than preacher as he wrote of beholding an African American man who could read the New Testament—something he considered quite remarkable in South Carolina.[190]

Meanwhile, the relentless and thorough destruction continued. Sherman's saboteurs destroyed attachments, tanks, sheds, sewers and every facility of the railroad. As Sherman's infantry pulled up the rails and ties, the First Michigan Engineers went to work on the "twist." The engineers had mastered the art of twisting the rails to frightening precision. It was a talent that made the men worth their weight in gold.[191] In a testimony to their work, a Yankee soldier would remark with a tinge of levity that the rails, nicknamed "Lincoln Gimlets," were now of use only to a junk dealer.[192]

All was not orderly and pleasant. A soldier of the 102nd Illinois recalled the frustration of marching and countermarching frequently throughout the day. Double booking with other units and wrong roads led to "savage swearing" throughout the ranks. Where follies in leadership failed, the smoke of burning property and railroad ties was suffocating as it "enveloped the whole country."[193] More and more, South Carolina was continuing to resemble a scene from Dante's *Inferno*.

Chapter 12

The Plantations Now Looked Desolate

Humans usually have two responses to approaching devastation: batten down the hatches or run for the hills. For those traveling in the wake of Sherman's columns, it seemed the latter was the prevailing sentiment. A wasteland of desolation awaited, leaving the homes and hearths of absent owners open to Sherman's men. While the destruction continued, the detached elements of the Fifteenth and Twentieth Corps were desperately battling to catch up from Sister's Ferry. We will begin our look with the latter, Major General John W. Geary's Second Division and Colonel James Selfridge's detached brigade.

Fortunately, the Savannah's high waters were receding. Despite the encouraging news, work parties would spend the better part of four days corduroying the road to the river. Occasionally, the labor turned deadly as the workmen struck torpedoes implanted along the road. Revealingly, Geary would later call the work "one of the greatest difficulty" owing to the risky torpedoes and taxing high waters.[194]

On February 4, Geary finally crossed the Savannah. Greeting him was a road submerged for over three miles as it passed Black Swamp. For Selfridge's men, the trip was over the very same roads they had sloshed through almost a week earlier. At least one New Yorker could see the flooding in relative terms. Although the road was in better shape than before, much of the road still remained under knee-deep water.[195]

Complicating matters was the addition of Kilpatrick's 250 wagons to Geary's own two-hundred-strong train. This new burden made corduroy efforts even harder. Geary sent most of his command through the swamp to vanquished Robertville. Barnum's Third Brigade was left to secure the expansive wagon train's passage through the swamp. Throughout the night and following day, 1,500 men labored to corduroy the road as Captain Abner Shipman of the Sixtieth New York recounted:

> *The duty required of the regiment on this day was far from agreeable, made so more particularly as the men of the regiment…were required to enter the swamps on either side of the road, where the water was in many places two and three feet deep, for the purpose of cutting poles and dragging them to the road to be used in corduroying, while other portions of the brigade placed the poles in the road.*

At noon, the work paid off as the head of the train finally emerged from the quagmire. If the work offered a tangible illustration of the "far from agreeable" work ahead, a nearby plantation offered a glimpse of the climate of destruction. A wrecked but still standing plantation called "The Manor" was found by some of Selfridge's men in deplorable condition, its absent secessionist owners condemning it to its fate. Apologetically, the perpetrators excused such abuses as a desire to see to it that such people suffered for bringing civil war on the country.

The column wasted little time to get back into motion by marching to Trowell's Crossroads, eight miles from Robertville. Fortunately for all, the roads had greatly improved. Likewise, the rain had subsided, and no Confederate resistance barred the road. This façade of safety was soon shattered, however, when a frightening discovery was found at nearby Trowell's farm.

Three Federal soldiers lay dead in the brush near the Trowell home. According to slaves, the men had been pointed out by Mr. Trowell to a band of Wheeler's cavalry who then shot down the doomed foragers in "cold blood." Geary placed Trowell under arrest as an accessory to the murders, had the dead men properly buried and ordered Trowell's home and property destroyed in retaliation. They were in South Carolina, and Geary's command had already seen their comrades slain by both torpedoes and invisible bands of Rebels. Yet, they had yet to meet even the most remote semblance of resistance.

On February 6, the column moved on to gamely contested but entirely destroyed Lawtonville. The entire march was a tour of devastation as the formerly rich country suffered a similar fate. The flight of local citizens and the earlier plundering of foragers had stripped the country bare. Distressingly, an onset of heavy rain began falling that evening, lasting throughout what was "anything but a comfortable night." It was an ominous omen of more hard work to come.

The following day, the column moved in rainfall that showed no signs of letting up. Once again, the roads turned to mush as the sounds of pioneers echoed through the trees. By noon, Geary's column reached the Coosawhatchie Swamp. What greeted Geary's men and wagon was yet another impassable mire. No bridges remained crossing the three-foot-deep swamp that stretched for over three hundred yards. Through this heavily timbered morass also ran Duck Branch, only complicating matters further.

Geary put six hundred men to work hacking down timber for a footbridge and to corduroy the submerged thoroughfare. Thoroughly saturated, the ground sunk like quicksand, forcing Federal pioneers to wade into the swamp to corduroy soft spots. In the midst of the steady rain, Federal pioneers found themselves pinning their corduroys to avert them floating away. Despite the constant stoppages, the work finally began to pay off as at 4:00 p.m., Geary began crossing. Geary's entire division, artillery and a considerable portion of his wagons passed the swamp throughout the night. Delayed by swamps, his column had only marched six and a half miles.

Geary's remarkable feat was tempered with the sobering realization that there were still over two hundred wagons left across the swamp. The trains were left in the charge of Selfridge's brigade, much to the chagrin of the Federal officer. Selfridge now found himself responsible for getting the lingering wagons across on his own. Toward that end, three hundred men were put to work. After seven arduous hours, Selfridge's pioneers finally finished after midnight. One weary Yankee recalled the end of the exhausting day as the men "raised their tents in the woods, wet to the skin, cold and hungry to get as much rest as possible before morning." The same soldier would go on to call it one of the worst days of fatigue and discomfort since stepping off from Savannah.[196]

The following day was par for the course as Selfridge's men struggled to move the train across the swamp and Duck Branch. Some wagons mired in the mud, forcing men to haul out the wagons as animals took fright. When wagons finally emerged from the swamp, the waterlogged road beyond was hardly better. For Selfridge's men, scarcely had a day been seen on the march that did not require corduroying. But, the column and trains were through the swamp, and the open, higher country lay ahead.

One way to cross a swamp—a fallen log. *Courtesy of the author.*

By the next morning, the column was once again moving for another quagmire, Buford's Bridge. Thirty minutes after Geary's column stepped off, a courier rode up. Three miles north of the Coosawhatchie Swamp, Sherman had made contact with his estranged portion of the Twentieth Corps. For Geary and Selfridge's beleaguered troops, contact with their long "lost" comrades—no matter how small—could not have come at a better time.

Geary pushed his command hard, crossing the Salkehatchie at Buford's Bridge by February 9. The lack of footbridges through the swamps forced the men to once again wade through the high waters. As the men finally gained dry ground, a soldier recalled feet that felt as if they were fifty pounds while their feet "churned" water out of soaked brogans. But, the men were across, and this time the prospect of dry land was far more promising.

As the column swung toward Blackville, things looked bright. For Geary's men, who had faced bad roads, poor forage and rainy weather for days, the eighteen-mile march to Blackville must have been paradise. The country looked higher and better than any they had covered, and Geary contentedly reported abundant forage for the first time. All was not a total utopia, however, as cold freezing weather induced some snow flurries on the already weary troops. Devastation and the charred remnants of houses served as a yardstick to their comrades' previous progress.[197] By 3:00 p.m. Geary's command halted their weary bones and went into camp. A mile ahead at Blackville, their comrades were at work destroying the railroad. The Twentieth Corps had been reunited.[198]

It was now the Fifteenth Corps's turn. Crossing the Savannah on the evening of February 4 was Major General John Corse's Fourth Division.[199] The first few miles into South Carolina looked ominous. Like Geary's before him, Corse's route lay directly through the three-mile expanse of Black Swamp. Remarkably, the roads once again had to be repaired. The hero of the fierce Battle of Allatoona Pass should be up for the challenge. Corse had once written off wounds in that encounter by wiring Sherman that he was "short of a cheekbone and one ear, but am able to whip all hell yet."[200] But a swamp took a different kind of soldiering.

Corse threw out three regiments to repair the road at daybreak, and by 3:00 p.m., the road was in enough shape to grind forward. Striking Robertville and the Lawtonville Road, Corse swung his command on the direct Hickory Hill Road. By February 7, the division reached the banks of the Coosawhatchie Swamp. Facing roads turned to mush by heavy rainfall, Corse later proudly recalled what he faced ahead:

> *The entire division was, as I may say, organized into a temporary pioneer corps, the men marching for miles with fence rails upon their shoulders with which to corduroy the swamps and quicksand roads before a wagon could pass over them, and in many instances performing the severest labor in water to their waists, remaining thus exposed until in many cases they were brought from the water in a cramped and spasmodic condition.*

Corse threw out the Seventh Iowa and Twelfth Illinois to repair the bridges and corduroy the wrecked road in a steady rain. An Iowa officer recounted the work as his men waded out into the surrounding swamps, dominated by at least six flowing channels, to find planks to repair the wrecked bridges. By four o'clock that afternoon, Corse's command was moving again, eventually halting at Hickory Hill. Less than a week before, their comrades had passed the same spot.

The arrival at Hickory Hill offered a chance to reconnect with the Right Wing somewhere to the north. Corse fired off a dispatch to Sherman, sounding every bit of a man exhausted by the "execrable" roads he had encountered. "I know not how anxious you may be to have me with you, but I assure you not more so than I am," he wrote while at the same time stating that if he could bridge the swamp, he would move heaven and earth to rejoin the Right Wing in two days. Corse clearly had had his feel of the Carolina swamps, and the sooner he was reunited with the Fifteenth Corps the better. But there were far more swamps to come.

The following morning Corse found familiar faces. A detachment of the Ninth Illinois Mounted Infantry was found passing through, escorting a wagon train. Offering a somber if not unnerving sight, the mounted men had been escorting wounded combatants of Rivers' Bridge. Corse joined up with his newfound comrades and marched the twelve miles to Whippy Swamp. In their journey that day, Corse's division had covered seven miles and crossed the Salkehatchie at Rivers' Bridge, site of the severe fight only six days before.[201] If the wagons that carried the wounded men failed to impress upon them the severity of that fight, surely the now empty Confederate entrenchments did not.

Chapter 13

The Most Complete Rout I Have
Ever Witnessed

With the pontoon laid at Sister's Ferry, the Fourteenth Corps under Major General Jefferson C. Davis remained to enter the state. More than most, the controversial Davis had a reason to despise South Carolina, having taken part in the defense of Fort Sumter when South Carolinians bombarded it to begin the "late unpleasantness." Now was his chance to do something about it.

By the night of February 5, virtually Davis's entire command was in South Carolina. Complications abounded; thus, it was not until February 10 that Davis's corps concentrated near already vanquished Barnwell.[202] The prosperous planters along the Savannah would pay dearly. In the words of a man of the Thirty-fourth Illinois, "Now was carried into execution the threats of our men in the ranks to make South Carolina regret the day she gave birth to Secession." Everywhere were signs of devastation. Every house, many of them mansions, was no more as earlier comrades ravaged the homes and hearths of the elite. Not all of the scenes of destruction were after the fact. An officer of the Fifty-second Ohio recalled that the scene of "conflagration right and left front, and rear, was like a patch from the eternal burning, the smoke of their runs ascends forever, or until they knock under." A howling wilderness and utter desolation marked the country, and ahead lay already desolated Barnwell.

The citizens of Barnwell watched Yankees once again march through what was left of their town. According to one Federal, the few remaining souls sat dressed in their best outside their homes, awaiting the second

Better late than never, Major General Jefferson C. Davis. *Courtesy of the Library of Congress.*

round of destruction. Fortunately, the newly arriving soldiers took at least some precautions against a repeat of Kilpatrick's occupation. The Second Minnesota was quickly deployed around town to protect the surviving property. A report circulating throughout the Yankee ranks that Barnwell had supplied the Confederacy's first volunteers may have helped encourage Kilpatrick's rampage and could spell more trouble in this second occupation.[203] The Minnesotans may have been the only defense the town had against the "execution" of the aforementioned Federal threats.

Ironically, one of the more memorable incidents came as an earlier Yankee taunt came true. One of those reputed "officers worse than the men" joined the roaming bummers in their deeds. Announcing that he would burn the town and "would like to see the guards who would stop him," the man seemed defiant. It was not until a Minnesotan leveled off his rifle ready to send him into eternity that he fled. Nevertheless, as the Fourteenth Corps left town the next day, fires could be seen breaking out in a dozen places. The Minnesotans' commander watched helplessly as his former ward was "no doubt totally destroyed" in the developing conflagration at "Burnwell."[204]

Such destruction continued to take Dantesque dimensions. A man of the 104th Illinois recalled the foragers returning to camp with abundant supplies. Such success was, he quipped, proof that something other than hell could be raised in South Carolina. The same witness, however, noted that the many conflagrations gave evidence that the infernal regions could just as easily dwell in the Palmetto State. One such conflagration raged as an ill-fated native tried to prevent the fire engulfing his home from spreading to his surrounding buildings and fences. With bitter sarcasm, a Yankee asked rhetorically how his home had taken to the flames.[205]

Resistance had temporarily lightened for Sherman's infantry. For Kilpatrick's cavalry, however, nothing could be further from the truth. When we last left the Federal horseman, his forces had just captured Blackville. Feinting on Augusta, Kilpatrick leaned west. On February 8, Colonel George E. Spencer's Third Brigade marched out with a four-hour head start toward Williston on the Augusta Road. In a twist of circumstance that would prove ironic, the Unionist First Alabama Cavalry led the advance.

Five miles out, two squadrons under Major Sanford Tramel struck a picket post manned by fellow Alabamans of Hagan's cavalry brigade of Allen's division. Predictably, the post was easily overrun, and the Rebels fell back through Williston. As they had at Blackville the day before, Rebel horsemen yielded yet another town with nothing more than a few feeble shots in opposition. Tramel halted his column and established the customary picket post a half mile west of town. As the balance of the regiment under Major Francis L. Cramer arrived and went into camp, the sound of gunfire from the direction of Tramel's picket post echoed in. Something was amiss outside of town. Just in case, a couple of squadrons were sent to its assistance.

His blood up as the gunfire increased, Tramel rushed forward with the rest of the regiment to find Hagan's troopers were fighting back. In one of those rare times in the war, Southerners battled each other at the picket post. With all of the First Alabama Cavalry now on the scene, Tramel's battalion drove Hagan's recovered troopers a mile and a half until the Rebels drew up into a strong position. Major Cramer would soon arrive on the scene to personally lead his regiment against their Alabama neighbors.

Meanwhile, Spencer prepared his brigade for a fight. He had obviously met a considerable force on the outskirts of Williston. While fighting raged,

Spencer ordered Major Christopher T. Cheek's Fifth Kentucky Cavalry to remain saddled until Cramer was heard from. A half an hour later and with a fight that seemed to become more furious by the minute, Cheek's regiment and a section of the Tenth Wisconsin Battery were rushed to Cramer's support. As a final step, Spencer ordered Major George H. Rader with his Fifth Ohio Cavalry to leave a battalion holding the town and wagons and to take the balance of his command to Cramer's assistance at a slow pace.

While his superior prepared, Cramer disposed his regiment for keeping Hagan's troopers on the run. Going wide, Cramer threw two parties with twenty men each on either flank of the Rebel line. With the balance making up his center, Cramer lunged forward. Pressed on flank and front, Hagan's troopers broke and fell back another half a mile. Cramer's troopers kept up the pressure, driving their secessionist neighbors from yet another position. Meanwhile, Cheek's Kentuckians caught up with their comrades. Spencer now had two regiments to overpower Hagan's struggling horsemen.

Hagan finally found a spot favorable to make a stand. If any position offered a chance to slow the Federals, White Pond would surely suffice. Hagan posted his men in a line of timber with open fields stretching along his front and White Pond guarding one of his flanks. His assailants would be forced to assault his position entirely exposed in the open field. All the while, Hagan's troopers had the advantage of the timber as cover from Spencer's clearly superior firepower. Perhaps it would be Lawtonville all over again.

Spencer ordered Cramer's men forward as skirmishers while putting Cheek's Kentuckians into a line of battle. Now in place, the entire line broke into a charge. Hagan's Alabamans managed only a single volley before shattering. The badly beaten troopers conceded not only ground but also every manner of hindrance to make their escape. Hats, rifles, haversacks, saddlebags and canteens were all discarded in a "most complete rout." Spencer pursued for five miles, scattering the rattled Alabamans into the swamps and woods.

In a testament to the severe beating Hagan's command endured, thirty Rebels, Hagan's brigade flag and four regimental flags were captured. This resounding rout of Hagan's brigade came at the cost of at least one Kentuckian dead and four others wounded. With his foe routed, Spencer retired back to Williston.[206] His "Tories" could sleep well knowing they had earned bragging rights over their neighbors.

Chapter 14

Only Those Who Were There Could Tell

It had been a long war that was seemingly approaching its last days. And yet, still Confederates opposed Sherman's advance almost daily. Such gallantry against overwhelming numbers must have brought wonderment as to its origins. The defiant women of the South seemed as good a culprit as any. The question still remained: as these foot soldiers of the homefront fled Sherman's path, would the will of their soldiers break as well?

Sherman's army was shifting, and behind burned bridges, Confederates were left powerless. With the Rebels momentarily blinded, a move toward Columbia was Sherman's plan. The Twentieth Corps began February 9 by moving west from Graham's to seize now "dilapidated" Blackville. Predictably, Williams's men were thrown to work destroying the railroad in and around the town. Once again the "all pervading smoke" from the destruction and stacks of burning fence rails made things miserable for the men as they worked.[207] Shifting west, Logan ordered the Fifteenth Corps out of their bivouacs the same day and, with two divisions, marched the eight miles to Graham's Turnout. Logan threw two divisions in position guarding the approach from the road to Holman's and Binnaker's Bridges. A couple of brigades were put to work smashing the railroad west of the town toward Blackville.

Pursuing intelligence, Hazen's Second Division moved on the Augusta Road to the Holman's Bridge–Augusta Road crossroads without opposition. From here, Hazen would push a force to Holman's Bridge to prepare for crossing the South Edisto. When the destruction near Graham's Turnout

The South Edisto at Holman's Bridge. *Courtesy of the author.*

was complete, the balance of the Fifteenth Corps would join him there. Meanwhile, the Seventeenth Corps also began its move to the west. Blair swung his command from Midway and moved on the Augusta Road to the crossing of the South Edisto at Binnaker's Bridge downstream of Holman's Bridge.[208]

By midday, the two vanguards arrived at their respective destinations. At Holman's Bridge, Hazen probed Colonel Theodore Jones's First Brigade toward the bridge. Shaking out the Fifty-seventh Ohio and Fifty-fifth Illinois as skirmishers, Jones found the usual impediments. The Federal position sat upon a bluff, towering above a cypress swamp covering the north side. It was this swamp that the now bridgeless road cut through.

A greater impediment was evident as the Yankees crept up closer to the river. Concealed by trees across the river, Confederate sharpshooters opened up an "extremely hot" fire making crossing a "hopeless" endeavor. Solidifying the pessimistic outlook, a Rebel sharpshooter killed Private James Ardinger and another wounded Private Samuel Gordon, both of the Fifty-seventh Ohio. Clearly, a way of outflanking the deadly sharpshooters was prudent.[209]

What the swamp concealed beyond its half-mile-wide expanse was Brigadier General Zachary Deas's entrenched brigade, 270-plus effectives.

Born in Camden, South Carolina, Deas moved to Mobile, Alabama, as a young man. Making his fortune as a cotton broker, Deas had now come full circle back to the state of his birth and the fiefdom of cotton.[210] As the tatter of musketry floated in from the swamps, Deas ironically found himself defending his native soil with a displaced brigade of Alabamans.

Concealed by the swamp, Jones cut an approach through the swamp to a point a mile and a half to three-quarters of a mile above the bridge. Through the opening, four companies of the Fifty-fifth Illinois were sent through and across the river via rafts and fallen trees. Unfortunately for the Yankees, so gamely wading the swamps along the river, the swamps across the river were just as expansive. Gains were fitful, as it was nearly a mile before anything resembling solid ground was reached.[211] By this time, nightfall halted their operations.[212]

One party of Yankees kept things interesting with a discovery a mile from the bridge. The small detachment crossed at least one channel in the swamp and waded through up to two-foot-deep water for several hours before reaching the main river. Even there it took constructing a raft from drifting logs to cross. When the raft lost its usefulness, the Yankees once again sank into waist-deep water. After such troubles, the small platoon found an oblivious camp of Confederate horsemen encamped no more than sixty rods away. Only a moatlike millrace thwarted a rash decision to charge the unsuspecting troopers. The situation defused, the party slinked back into the swamp, found a rare dry spot and hunkered down for a frosty night. Meanwhile, developments to the east at Binnaker's Bridge made their ramblings moot.[213]

Leading the Seventeenth Corps to Binnaker's Bridge was Mower's First Division. Mower arrived within a half mile of the bridge by midday and quickly ordered Tillson's brigade forward in a column of regiments. Surveying the scene, Mower found his men occupying a high bluff overlooking the river. Once again, the Confederates had burned the bridge, something that gave Mower reason to lament. The river spanned over fifty yards, while cypress swamps submerged the riverbanks for a considerable distance above and below the bridge. Across the river, Confederates held rifle pits with a battery of artillery. Relieving the Ninth Illinois Mounted Infantry, Tillson's skirmishers took their place in a brisk skirmish with their Southern counterparts. As the fight escalated, the First Michigan Artillery, Battery C, added its own weight to the fray.

Manning the rifle pits across the river were Stovall's and Jackson's Georgia brigades from Clayton's division and Stevenson's corps under Colonel Abda

Johnson. All in all, five hundred Confederates, bolstered by Kanapaux's artillery, lay ahead. Jackson's late-arriving, diminutive brigade of fewer than one hundred troops offered a painful reminder of the dire nature of Confederate resistance along the Edistos in 1865. Among their ranks, young Major Robert Newton Hull watched over his men of the Sixty-sixth Georgia. The nephew of Lieutenant General William Hardee, Hull knew well the low morale that hung over his skeletal command. In a letter to his brother-in-law, he captured the pessimistic feelings of his command:

> My men are completely demoralized, and I fear when the crisis comes they will be found wanting. Nevertheless, I shall do my duty. "Coming events," tis said, "cast their shadows before," and even now I feel a presentiment of evil. Perhaps I shall never see another sun set, but if I fall it will be with my face to the foe.[214]

Confederate soldiers were not alone in preparing for Sherman's legions. Henrietta Barnes, driven from Atlanta by Sherman's forces, had come to the home of a relative less than a mile from the bridge. For days, Barnes looked on the destroyed bridge as a hopeful sign that Sherman's marauders would stay beyond the river's dark waters. However, the sounds of artillery and skirmish fire dampened such hopes as the afternoon wore on.

Even Mower got caught up in the hysteria of the developing fight. The impetuous chieftain responded to Rebel taunts by rising up in his stirrups and shaking his fist at his cocky adversaries. An aide recalled the spirited officer giving the only hint at his motives by exclaiming, "God man, wouldn't you like to wade in there with a saber?"[215] Another of Mower's men recalled him seizing an overcurious slave and hurling him down the river bluff.[216] With such displays, the Rebels had indications that this was not a Federal officer content with staying across the river.

Despite Mower's longing to wade saber in hand, crossing the river would take both audacity and ingenuity. Yankees went to work forming rafts; however, deadly Rebel rifle and artillery fire hampered their efforts. The accurate fire of Federal artillery evened the score, driving Kanapaux's Carolinians back up the road. Confederate fire had its own effect, killing Private Jeremiah Gardner and wounding another Yankee gunner. While gunners sparred, a fortuitous discovery turned the tide.

One hundred and fifty yards below the bridge, attentive skirmishers noticed a fence across the river that came nearly to the riverbank. Correctly surmising that the ground there must be higher than the surrounding swamp

"A crossing second in importance to the Salkehatchie": the South Edisto at Binnaker's Bridge. *Courtesy of the author.*

bottoms, Federals hacked out a road and began constructing rafts. Even those rafts abandoned earlier were of use, as a man waded through the icy waters to catch one as it floated downriver. Wherever their raft's origin, a squad was ferried over to stretch a rope for a pontoon bridge.

Out of range and sight of the defenders, Tillson threw across three companies of the Thirty-second Wisconsin. There they received an instant preview of what was to come as the first twenty yards lay submerged. Around five o'clock that evening, the pontoon was laid five hundred yards below the bridge and the rest of Tillson's men thrown across, with Montgomery's Second Brigade just behind. For Montgomery's shuffling men, the danger of Rebel artillery was still present. As the men moved down to the pontoon, shells from Kanapaux's guns zeroed in. One of the exploding shells landed near the column, severely wounding First Lieutenant John R. Casson of the Twenty-fifth Wisconsin in the hand. Like at Rivers' Bridge, Confederate guns were once again giving the regiment grief.

Meanwhile, in the swamps complications continued. Tillson's men swung three-quarters of a mile to the right to turn the Confederate flank. Greeting

The South Edisto swamps. *Courtesy of the author.*

the Yankees as they turned toward the mainland was a swampy quagmire extending as far as the eye could see. More disturbingly, the temperature had dropped as nightfall approached. All around lay a dark, icy soup of mud and water. It was this barrier that barred them from the now seemingly elusive mainland. Mower's men had crossed the river but now found themselves in the middle of a swamp with daylight vanishing by the second. In search of a way out, Captain DeGress and Captain Bryant, of Mower's and Tillson's staff respectively, ventured into the darkness ahead.

Luckily, their trek was successful, and the Yankees moved for the glimmering hope of dry land. Progress was slow, with nightfall making the already arduous task even more difficult. As the Yankees moved through sometimes waist-deep swamp, men swung cartridge belts around their necks to save their ammunition. Motivated by the late hour and the cold air, others moved knapsacks on their shoulders to avoid drenching their blankets and other vitals.[217] On a day that had been cold from the start, the prospect of spending all night shivering with wet blankets was hardly appealing. Later Federals would recount the shouts of "grab a root!" as men stumbled along, tripped up by submerged roots.[218] However, even some of the most menacing swamps that the Palmetto State could offer only slowed, not halted, the progress.

Meanwhile, back at the Rebel entrenchments, excitement flourished. Henrietta Barnes recalled a Confederate officer racing into the house just before sundown and informing the gathered flock of local civilians that Sherman's men were crossing the river. Barnes's fears soon abounded as she watched the Confederates begin their retreat:

> *The sun was just sinking as our men began their retreat. Poor fellows! How sad and forlorn they looked as they filed slowly by the gate. I stood upon the piazza and watched them with the tears rushing down my cheeks—the first and only time my courage quite forsook me during the whole of that dreadful time…I gazed upon this forlorn band of worn and defeated heroes who had nobly born the brunt of a hundred battles and must yet retreat ignominiously before the advancing hosts of the enemy and leave the helpless women and children. I could well imagine their feelings, as with bowed heads, tattered clothing and pinched hungry looking faces they passed with slow, monotonous tramp, tramp, tramp along the road.*

Around 8:00 p.m., Mower's amphibians finally struck open field. Sheltered in the woods, Tillson's men noticed the picket fires of an oblivious Confederate camp. Their hike had placed them somewhere on the Rebel left flank. Seriously hampering their attack was that the swamp crossing had broken up Tillson's command. Consequently, only a company faced the front while three more watched the left flank. Like the near miss upstream, it was the ideal time for misfortune to strike as a Rebel battle line, covered by skirmishers, moved toward the small Yankee force.

Commanding the skirmish line was Major Robert Hull. We remember Hull as the young Confederate officer who entertained such uneasiness about the coming fight. Hull's pedigree would certainly not have hurt in getting a far less hazardous duty on that cold February night. However, like a gladiator of old, Hull led his men out into the darkness. Wisely, Tillson admonished his men to lie down and only return fire when ordered. It was an order that was soon to come. Hull led his men forward to within fifty feet of the prone Federals before challenging the dark figures in the tree line.

No response forthcoming, a Southern voice barked, "Fire." Rebel rifles erupted into the darkness, their flash likely illuminating their owners. His bluff called, Tillson gave his own highly anticipated order, and his troops returned fire. As predicted, Hull's men broke. In a vain attempt to rally his men, Hull threw himself behind them, encouraging them to hold fast. The young major's valor was in vain, as a Federal ball hit Hull in the left temple.[219] Struck by a seemingly mortal wound, Hull collapsed while his men fled, abandoning three of their comrades and their badly wounded commander.

Henrietta Barnes, overcome with anxiety, hustled to one of the retreating Rebel columns. Begging for news, her query was answered excitedly by a Confederate officer. "For God's sake, Madame, go back to the house, unless you want your head taken off by a sharp-shooter. They are right up the lane, not a half-mile away. Do you not hear the firing?" Barnes hurried back into the house. She and the other frightened ladies could only await the arrival of Sherman's legions, whose rifles could be heard getting closer and closer.

After Montgomery's leading regiment arrived, Tillson finally scattered the Rebel rear guard through the woods in confusion. One of Kanapaux's abandoned caissons was even snatched up by the advancing skirmishers.[220] Meanwhile, as Henrietta Barnes looked out of her window for signs of the approaching blue surge, her eyes caught a glimpse of a lone soldier, his rifle and uniform making his identity certain, moving through the moonlit yard. Slowly and weary of unseen Rebels, the soldier opened a side gate and entered the yard surrounding the house. He was the first of many.

Moments later, Federal troops—their trousers frozen stiff—arrived. Trying to head off mayhem, Barnes requested a guard. Hardly a gentleman, one Federal responded, "Ladies the devil, had it not been for them egging the men on, the war would have been squelched years ago." Barnes recalled the crackle of Yankee uniforms as they moved about in their plunder driven mayhem. "The most terrible scene pictured in the inferno could not compare with it," described the pandemonium as Mower's men ravaged the plantation. "Nothing seeming sacred from their vile touch." Yankees tore into bureaus, trunks and closets while scattering about and trampling their contents. Meanwhile, in the yard cows lowed, pigs squealed, lambs bleated and fowl squawked as Yankees chased the potential meals for slaughter.

As their "foraging" wore down, Yankees pragmatically sought to dry themselves. Men cursed, jostled and crowded as they squeezed closer to a fireplace's alluring warmth. Shortly, puddles emerged as frozen uniforms thawed. While men congratulated each other for the day's accomplishments, steam rose as heat met the soaked soldiers. Surrounded by such a scene, we can excuse Mrs. Barnes's association of the night's turmoil with Dante's treatise on hell.

Walking amid the chaos, Mrs. Barnes's attention was drawn to a conversation. Describing the earlier skirmish, two Union soldiers talked with admiration of the bravery of a young Confederate officer who "rushed on us like a tiger, cheering his men on to the last, and died with the war cry still ringing from his lips." Barnes's sympathy turned to agony as the Yankees disclosed the soldier's name, "Major Hulsey." Having a relative by that name, Barnes entreated the two officers to bring her kinsman into the house.

A half hour later, the dying young officer was brought in and laid across a mattress. A short flash of relief came upon Barnes, as she did not recognize the man's face. As she would shortly learn, he was, in fact, Major Hull. Barnes and Captain L.M. Dayton of Sherman's staff tried desperately to save Hull's life before it left him with "a few hoarsely muttered, disconnected sentences and a nervous twitching of the muscles of the lips." Like two of his brothers, the young "tiger" Hull had paid the ultimate price for his country's cause. A long way from his Georgia home, he was buried under a spreading live oak near the plantation gate.[221]

Hope of a fleeting Federal presence evaporated as Mower's men began entrenching a mile and a half beyond the crossing. With the Confederate skedaddle, a pontoon bridge was laid and the causeway repaired. Around midnight, men of Force's division had interrupted supper and emptied coffee cups in mind as they glimpsed Mower riding along near the bridge. A traveling monument to his great accomplishment, Mower's frozen overcoat, like those of his men, crackled.[222] In a fitting tribute, his superior, Howard, lauded that "only those who were there could tell" of Mower's great feat that day.[223]

Throughout the rest of the night and morning, the Seventeenth Corps crossed the South Edisto. It was a feat that was far from routine, as Blair called the crossing "second only in importance and the difficulties" to crossing the mighty Salkehatchie. Casualties were also second to that fight, as three Federals were killed and seven more wounded.[224] Despite the bitter cold, a swollen river, swamps and desperate Confederates, the Seventeenth Corps had crossed yet another river. It truly was a feat fit only for an army of amphibians rather than men.

Chapter 15

As If a Knife Was Cutting the Flesh

Mower's nocturnal crossing was the rule rather than the exception. The same conditions could be expected from now on. This brand of fighting was here to stay. For Mower, the South Carolina swamps perhaps left their deadly mark. Five years later, Mower would die a relatively young man from pneumonia. It is not a leap to wonder if his swamp-fighting days may have contributed to his weakened constituency.

Despite the overwhelming task before him, Confederate Major General Stevenson monitored developments with methodical care. On the night of February 9, Stevenson fired off a dispatch to Hardee in Charleston recounting the skirmishing on the South Edisto. For Hardee, this routine report was far more personal than he may have even known. While Stevenson composed the report, Hardee's nephew, Major Hull, was fighting and dying at obscure Binnaker's Bridge. Hardee's own personal loss against Sherman grew even deeper when his son died fighting Mower's division at Bentonville, North Carolina, over a month later.

Hoping to rally a defense, Stevenson sent off a courier toward Binnaker's Bridge. It was a trip that would be cut short. Approximately ten miles from Orangeburg, the courier met Johnson's command. Incredibly, Johnson was intoxicated. His incapacitation led his subordinates to appoint Lieutenant Colonel J.C. Gordon as temporary commander. Gordon reported the Federals had crossed the river in considerable force and that his men were now falling back toward Orangeburg in confusion.

Despite the hasty withdrawal, Johnson had taken the time to inform both Deas and Brigadier General Joseph Palmer at Cannon's Bridge of

The hero of the Salkehatchie and South Edisto: Major General Joseph Mower. *Courtesy of the Library of Congress.*

the situation. Deas, in turn, forwarded the news to his subordinate Colonel Carter whose brigade held Duncan's Bridge upstream. Outflanked, Palmer's division fell back toward Orangeburg while Deas's division withdrew toward Columbia. Finally, Dibrell's and Brigadier General Robert Anderson's cavalry brigades, at Guignard's Bridge and Pine Log Bridge respectively, retired.[225] Mower's desire to wade "in there with saber" had effectively forced the abandonment of the South Edisto.

Stevenson intended to hold the North Edisto as long as possible. The delay was important as valuable stores were being collected beyond the river at Orangeburg. Stevenson wished to gain as much time as possible to move these stores beyond the Congaree River. The North Edisto was tough to defend. Moving upstream, the river left its confluence with the Edisto and South Edisto first in a northerly direction, paralleling the Cannon Bridge Road. Just shy of Orangeburg, the river turned to the west and continued its course. It was this higher, east–west span of the North Edisto where Stevenson positioned the majority of his forces.

As If a Knife Was Cutting the Flesh

On its other span, Rowe's Bridge added problems. It provided the major crossing on the north–south span of the river. With its position between the upper crossings of the North Edisto and the Edisto confluence, this crossing was the most critical point of the North Edisto line. A bold movement across Rowe's Bridge would threaten both Stevenson's left flank at Orangeburg and McLaws's right flank/rear at Branchville.

Stevenson put his men into position. Anderson's and Dibrell's cavalry brigades were posted farther up the North Edisto watching the higher bridges on Stevenson's right. Moving downstream and on the direct routes to Columbia, Deas's and Carter's brigades were posted. Just above Orangeburg, Palmer's brigade entrenched to guard Shilling's Bridge. Stovall's and Jackson's rattled brigades continued to Orangeburg where, with Kanapaux's Battery, they were entrenched along the low hill fronting the bridge over the North Edisto. Meanwhile, Brigadier General Edmund Pettus moved his brigade to Rowe's Bridge and began preparing for a defense. In a final attempt to cover the North Edisto, the detached Fifth Tennessee Cavalry was ordered to Stevenson's support.[226]

After the previous day's skirmishes, the Fifteenth Corps had a good idea of what it faced in crossing at Holman's Bridge. On February 10, five boats needed for a bridge were sent downstream to Logan. By 9:00 a.m., Colonel Theodore Jones's First Brigade had crossed the river. In a hardly unusual scene, over three-quarters of a mile of corduroying were required to pass Hazen's troops through the swamp beyond. Undeterred, Hazen's entire division began crossing around 4:00 that afternoon and took a position guarding the Columbia Road. Finished with their railroad work, the rest of the corps would cross the following day. Meanwhile, there was more positive news. Corse's Fourth Division had come up near Graham's Turnout. The hard-luck division, hampered by swamps and rivers for days, had covered twenty-two miles to close the gap.[227]

Corse's men were not the only new arrivals. As we will recall, we left the Twentieth Corps on February 9 as Geary's Second Division and Selfridge's brigade joined it near Blackville. There would be no rest for the weary new arrivals. Early on February 10, Selfridge's brigade marched seven miles to the South Edisto at Duncan's Bridge. Along the way, one New Yorker recalled passing through what "might have been Blackville."[228] Once again, the past tense is revealing, especially considering the village's alleged "secesh proclivities."[229] Around 10:00 the reconnaissance reached the crossing, effortlessly running off a small observation party of Rebels.

The name Duncan's Bridge is a misnomer, as six bridges made up its entire crossing. Of these, the Confederates had destroyed the two bridges over the river and another for good measure. Earthen causeways three-quarters of a mile long connected the six bridges over the swamp. Consequently, the overall crossing stretched over a mile. Each of these bridges and causeways would need to be repaired or corduroyed to get the rest of the corps and its wagons across the river. After building footbridges across the river, the Yankees ventured up the causeway in search of solid ground. Eventually, the thoroughfare emerged from the swamp into an open field ringed by a line of Rebel earthworks. Fortunately, Carter's small brigade no longer garrisoned its parapets. Taking advantage, Selfridge brought over the rest of his brigade in case the Rebels returned.

By the afternoon, the bridges were at least repaired enough for infantry. In fact, Selfridge's command would soon have company as Geary brought his division over. For the two commands, which had so recently battled the elements together on their march from Sister's Ferry, their bivouac was probably a less-than-charming reunion. Seeing each other may have been a reminder of other troubles. If that reminder did not suffice, another reminder of those murky swamps was coming shortly.

History does not record Selfridge's feelings when, the next day, he and Geary were once again tasked with corduroying through a hellish swamp. Only a few days had passed since Selfridge felt abandoned by Geary at the Coosawhatchie. Poetic justice was now in effect as both commands were forced to work together. Personalities aside, there was a great deal of work to be done with a lot at stake. The entire corps wagon train waited across the river at Blackville. There they would remain until a thoroughfare was laid from the newly rebuilt bridge.

The manpower dedicated to the task illustrated the sheer size of the undertaking. Selfridge put six hundred of his men to work until midday. Geary put almost half of his five thousand men to work as well. Deep channels and fourteen water passages varying from twelve to sixty feet wide compounded the usual difficulties. Difficulties and all, the causeways and bridges were repaired in time to see the corps wagon train and Jackson's division cross the river by nightfall.[230] Jackson's arrival was particularly poignant for Selfridge's men. In the words of one of their number, the men felt "lost" during their separation from their "old Red Star Division."

Even amid these pressing matters, there were moments of hilarity. Seeing a house just across the river with a liberal complement of fowl, a half a dozen men of the 123rd New York made a beeline. Even the presence of a few Confederate horsemen didn't deter them as they converged on the house, took fire and returned it right back. The Rebels yielded the abode and a leftover cake or two. Taking advantage, the Yankees took to chasing the petrified fowl in search of a "royal breakfast." Flying clubs sometimes clanked shins, but sure enough some fowls were carried back to camp. Much to their consternation, the sometimes painful effort of catching and cooking the birds was a waste. Disgustingly one man lamented, "They might just as well have boiled an old army shoe…for the chickens were too tough to eat."[231]

This tough break aside, there were happier foraging efforts. One man recalled an "abundance" of food that made for very little grumbling for men who had spent all day working in the swamp. For his own camp, fresh pork was just the remedy for his "cold, wet, tired" comrades. In an obvious understatement, our correspondent noted the foraged swine "tasted fine."[232] One can well imagine it did after a day of such hard work.

While Geary's men worked, Ward's division had a similar mission at Guignard's Bridge.[233] There Ward was to repair that bridge for the eventual passage of the Fourteenth Corps and cavalry. The First Michigan Engineers took time out from railroad smashing to lend a hand. Stepping off from Williston, Ward's division marched the twelve miles to the bridge on February 11. There the bridge was found destroyed by the now absent Confederates. Securing the crossing, the Eighty-fifth Indiana was thrown across while other elements of Dustin's brigade went to work gathering materials to rebuild the wrecked bridge. With material and security on hand, the night was spent rebuilding the bridge.

The next morning, Ward's men emerged from frost-covered blankets to find a discouraging sight. The swollen river had claimed all that could be seen. A man of the 102nd Illinois noted revealingly that the river appeared more swamp than stream. Water, anywhere from one to three feet deep, stretched a quarter of a mile wide with a thick forest of cypress trees and underbrush standing like silent sentinels in the black water.[234] More disturbing, the rebuilt bridge was an island, as the river had literally "outgrown" the wooden thoroughfare. Now, over two-thirds of the crossing would have to be waded.

Stripping off shoes and rolling up trousers, men went in. As they sloshed through the waist-deep waters, Yankee bodies shattered a crust of ice a quarter of an inch thick. One unfortunate soul of the Thirty-third Massachusetts vividly described the painful ordeal: "It seemed at every step as if a knife was cutting the flesh; everybody screamed with the pain, and the chorus of shouts was so funny that everybody had to laugh in turn."[235]

Levity was far from the norm with some men, as the cold waters "almost paralyzed" them as they sunk into the river's grip. Emerging from the icy waters, many men were "used up," building huge rail-fueled fires on the north bank to recover.[236]

In spite of the "severe" difficulties, Ward's entire division got across safely and marched unchecked until dropping bivouac three miles from the North Edisto crossing of Jeffcoat's Bridge. Three miles to their north, Geary's newly arrived Second Division would spend the remaining afternoon in a hot fight.

Chapter 16

The Men of This Army
Surprise Me Every Day

Recklessness, endurance and spirit certainly characterized the exploits so far. It would take more of the same to keep the momentum rolling forward. Like their comrades to the west, the men of the Right Wing found themselves across the South Edisto in full force by February 11. Despite their successes, the customary preparations like scouting still remained.

Reports of scouts were mixed. Some were encouraging as Rebels were nowhere to be found. Just as encouraging, the roads were found in good shape. For once, the men of the Right Wing should be able to march on roads that didn't swallow up their brogans and wagons. Also, their bellies would receive their due reward as plenty of forage lay along their route. In fact, the abundance was so notable that Howard issued an order that all empty wagons be filled with foraged supplies for the hard trips through barren country to come. It seemed their luck had changed. However, all was not peachy. Rumors abounded of Rebel resistance ahead as Stevenson's entire corps was waiting near Orangeburg.[237] Unfortunately for those few souls still under the tattered banners of the Confederacy, the "corps" now consisted of merely a few thousand men.

The Seventeenth Corps's column started for Orangeburg in the early morning hours of February 11. By 6:30 a.m., the clatter of hooves from the beasts of the Ninth Illinois Mounted Infantry echoed through the swamps as the horsemen crossed the South Edisto and took their place in advance of Blair's long column. Following the horsemen, Force's division led the column toward Orangeburg.[238] Just ahead, mounted foragers clopped up the road in search of plunder. Like at Midway, the scavengers served an unintended purpose. Clashing with mounted Rebels, the foragers drove them back to the safety of their main force.

Raising them reinforcement for reinforcement, the Ninth Illinois Mounted Infantry rushed to the front. The Yankee mounted men struck the Southerners with their usual fury. Overcome, the Federal rush was too strong as the Confederates retired toward Orangeburg. The Rebels reined in behind a barricade about two miles south of the river and about three and a half miles from Orangeburg to delay the tide.

A local girl recalled an awkward discovery of the Confederate barricade by a body of Yankee horsemen. After asking how far ahead the "Rebels" were, their enquiry was answered suddenly as balls whizzed by from the barricade a half mile ahead. The young lady recalled with glee the sight as "those Yankees" wheeled their horses about and ran through the woods back to their comrades.[239] Such hasty withdrawals were hardly one sided. With the infantry now coming up, the surging blue wave emptied the Confederates from the barricade.

For Rebels falling back toward Orangeburg, the road turned abruptly to the left where the Cannon Bridge Road intersected the road from Binnaker's Bridge. Running roughly parallel to the river, the terrain became considerably more like usual. Swamps chopped up the road into six crossings. For the retreating Confederates, leaving behind a trail of smoke and wrecked bridges would considerably delay an advance on Orangeburg just ahead.

Reaching the swamp, Force threw the Twentieth Ohio ahead to push the Rebels up the narrow causeway. Rushing at the double quick, the buckeyes drove the tattered gray figures hard. Near the river, the road turned abruptly to the right, yet onward Force's vanguard rushed. The pursuit was so rapid that the Confederates fell back across the river without a single one of the swamp bridges destroyed.[240] It must have all seemed eerily similar to another fight nine days before.

Pride was not the only casualty, as two Rebels lay dead in the smoke-enveloped swamp. Another man fell victim to a Federal ball and collapsed near the bridge. Six Rebels, unable to escape the Federal rush, found themselves in the custody of their midwestern adversaries. However, Force's vanguard had little time to savor their success. Ahead lay the river and whatever it may bring.

Clenching their weapons and artillery lanyards tight, Stovall's and Jackson's Georgians and Kanapaux's South Carolinians crouched in fortifications along the north bank of the river. In the swamp to their front, the scattered sounds of musketry and frantic shouts of heavily pressed comrades chilled the very blood that coursed through their veins. A mix of relief and dread must have drifted along the line as retreating comrades fled across the bridge and back into their own lines. Whatever was across the river was coming their way.

As Force's skirmishers came into view, artillery carefully concealed behind a parapet of earth and cotton bales roared. Joining in, Confederate infantry opened fire from the protection of their earthen shields.[241] Abandoning the causeway for the swamp, the Ohioans went into the motions. Like an unwinding cord, the Yankees stretched along the riverbank above and below the bridge. Up to their knees and hips in water, the Federals' impetuosity brought them into a sharp firefight with the Georgians across the river.[242]

What they developed was an extensive line of rifle pits that extended as far as the eye could see. Equally daunting, the two Rebel guns—as their heavy fire gave clear testament—totally swept the causeway as far back as the bend. From that point to the bridge, the South Carolina gunners offered shell, canister and shot to any Federals foolish enough to occupy the causeway. Force's advance, faced with intense musketry and artillery fire, halted in its tracks. It seemed like Rivers' Bridge all over again.

Held up, Force's men did at least command the bridge. Countering the Rebel artillery, a battery of Smith's division was brought up with that object and shelling the Confederate works in mind.[243] The result was a classic standoff with enough firepower in place to make a move for the bridge quite bloody. Consequently, both sides were content to remain where they were for the time being. With both sides stationary, the rest of the afternoon dissolved into a sniping game. All in all, both sides kept up just enough mischief to keep the other planted firmly in place.

Behind the racket, Force was busy finding a way to outflank the Rebels. Throughout the afternoon, details diligently scoured the river for just such a crossing point. Although several candidates were found, a winner was found downstream by a detachment of the Thirtieth Illinois. At this point, an open field extended all the way to the river. The opposite bank there appeared to be bordered by the characteristic wide swamp that fronted Orangeburg. More encouragingly, the point looked to be unwatched by Confederates. A crossing here could work.

Meanwhile, sounds trickled into the Yankee lines. Major Osborne recalled cheers and locomotive whistles across the river. The arriving trains could have been part of the evacuation of stores. As for the cheers, Confederates may have relished that their sharp defense had held the bridge. Considering

The North Edisto fronting Orangeburg. *Courtesy of the author.*

their recent rough handling on the South Edisto, it must have been pleasant to have no sudden Yankee surprises emerging from the swamps. Possibly another source of the cheers was news that Brigadier General Pettus's 380-man brigade was en route to aid in Orangeburg's defense.

The darkness brought about a night remembered for its numbing cold. A man of the Twelfth Wisconsin noted that the frigid air was enough to form ice on the swamp. Thinking of comrades skirmishing along the river, he would note humorously that the men up to their armpits in the swamps experienced a "cold bath." It is worthy to note that this was the same night that would leave the icy hell for Ward's division the following day at Guignard's Bridge.

All was not discomfort. Perhaps our witness had the disagreeable weather in mind as the regiment dropped into bivouac an hour before sundown. Finding a line of slave cabins, the men quickly dismantled the structures to make bunks with nearby dry grass as bedding. After a hearty supper, the men climbed into their "unusually comfortable" bunks for a good long night of sleep. Time would tell if it would be a lasting comfort.[244]

The quest for comfort was hardly limited. Mary McMichael and several female companions were rudely interrupted as a group of Federal foragers surrounded their home. Capturing the small party of Rebels holed up inside, Federals next went after the edible creatures in the yard. As one flighty guinea flew to the top of the chimney, a perturbed but witty Yankee announced, "Stay there you Rebel, I want you for my wedding dinner, for some day I am coming back to one of these Rebel girls." Such an odd courting technique was disturbing coming from the armed Federals growing exponentially in the area.[245]

Meanwhile, while shivering combatants contemplated more comfortable locales and their own Yankee girls back home, sounds of work drifted in from the bridge. The Yankees picketing the swamp opened fire toward the racket. Suddenly, the bridge burst into a fireball. As the flames roared, a lone Southerner leapt up on the glowing bridge. Immediately, Yankee fire cut down the unfortunate saboteur. Apparently, a small party used the cover of a small ravine to slip from their rifle pit to underneath the bridge. From there, they ignited the bridge.

The act's sheer audacity was matched only by its tragic desperation. In a testament to the Rebel hopelessness, the brave Rebel lad's death had been in vain. The bridge was only partially damaged. Furthermore, the bridge

A walking bridge marks the site of the original bridge at Orangeburg. *Courtesy of the author.*

had been rendered insignificant by the discovery of crossings elsewhere. Unbeknownst to Stevenson's defenders, the Federals planned on crossing somewhere on their flank.

By nightfall, Howard had arrived on the scene and got things moving. Blair was ordered to withdraw Force's division from the swamp. Smith's division would take their place to support batteries thrown into place overnight while pinning the Rebels in place. With the balance of his corps, Blair would outflank Stevenson. It was a script pulled straight from Pocotaligo. The only questions that remained were where to cross and whether Stevenson waited around for the denouement.

Sherman answered one of the questions. After Force reported the promising crossing point downstream, Uncle Billy quickly responded. "Yes, the lower place is the place to cross. Make your crossing there, your feint at the bridge, your diversion above."[246] The main shock force of Force's and Mower's divisions would cross downstream. During the night, Force put his men to work carving a road there in preparation.

"Pack up!" announced a voice as the men of the Twelfth Wisconsin were unceremoniously awakened from their pleasant slumber. His good sleep ruined, at least one man probably was representative of most as he stepped off "mad as a hornet." Ten minutes later, the sounds of musketry rolled in from their front. Anticipating marching straight into a fight, the men were no doubt relieved when the firing ceased, and they turned right into an old field. Before long, after dropping into camp, they were asleep again.[247] As part of Force's flanking column, they would need their rest for whatever tomorrow would bring.

Aiding the heavy juggernaut, Howard hoped to keep Stevenson honest with a simultaneous diversion on Rowe's Bridge. After their skirmishing south of town, the Ninth Illinois Mounted Infantry was dispatched to that crossing, ten miles away down Cannon Bridge Road. The bridge had received quite a deal of attention from Stevenson as his men retired from the South Edisto, thus was still not far from his mind. On February 11, pickets gazed off over the black waters two miles above the bridge. They had likely been warned of a large body of Yankees somewhere beyond the river. This in mind, the appearance of blue coats could be the first signs of a Yankee crossing.

Alarmingly, a detachment of horsemen came into view crossing the river. In panic, the pickets fled, with their warnings causing alarm for those along their path. News of this Federal crossing would surely mean that both Stevenson and McLaws must immediately abandon their entrenchments

The linchpin of the North Edisto: Rowe's Bridge. *Courtesy of the author.*

along the river. Fortunately, the alarm was unfounded. The dreaded "Federal" horsemen were actually a detachment of returning Confederate cavalry. Ironically, the troopers were attempting to sniff out just such a Yankee move for which they were mistaken.

Despite reassurances, Yankees did remain along Cannon Bridge Road. Rowe's Bridge sat less than a mile east of the road and roughly halfway between Orangeburg and the road's namesake. The heavy skirmishing upstream at Orangeburg had depleted the already thin garrison. Pettus's brigade had moved to aid in the defense upstream. Thus, the only defenders who remained posted defiantly in its entrenchments were the Fifth Tennessee Cavalry under Captain W.W. Lillard. As an early warning, pickets were posted along the river. Although the bridge had been destroyed, Lillard's best line of defense was Federal apathy. His small command certainly could not hold off any determined attempt to cross.

Lillard's men would have little time to ponder such thoughts. Hostile figures appeared across the river. The dismounted Yankees slogged through the swamp, using their superior firepower to drive the pickets from the riverbank and into the entrenchments. Unlike the false alarm, these "Yankees" added the crackle of rifles to the shock and awe of their sudden appearance. And unlike before, these were not a returning Rebel detachment.

Interestingly enough, Lillard's isolated position prevented him from learning much. All that Lillard could learn was that a considerable body of Federals was now sparring with his paper-thin line from across the river. All appearances were that they did not choose to remain there for long. To the beset captain, it was only a matter of time before the Federals overwhelmed his regiment. Yankee apathy now seemed off the table. But for all the worry, the Illinoisans had no intention of crossing there.

Ten miles to Lillard's north, a development made his own predicament mild. On the morning of February 12, a section of pontoon bridge was sent to Force approximately a mile below the Orangeburg Bridge. Around 11:00 a.m., the arduous task of laying the bridge was begun. Within a few hours, Force's division had crossed the prefabricated crossing to the north side of the river. Or in the words of one Federal soldier, the pontoon bridge mostly crossed the stream. It took adding several old scow boats to cover the final distance. Even this patchwork arrangement fell short. Impervious Yankees jumped off the bridge into the frigid river to complete the crossing.[248]

Far from home free, Force's men continued their trek by going through the thick swamp bordering the river. The usual dynamics of crossing were at play as Yankees sloshed, slashed and waded their way through. Whatever deficiencies Stevenson may have had in numbers, the swamps made up for with its own natural impediments. Difficulties aside, Force's entire division was across the North Edisto.

Meanwhile, Federal pyrotechnics abounded at the Orangeburg Bridge. Federal artillery pieces emplaced during the night were steady at work. Perhaps Force's men smiled as they heard the distant firing. It could only mean Yankee guns and skirmishers were keeping the Rebels occupied upstream. With such a display occurring, one may not blame Stevenson if he was somewhat distracted.

Rebel skirmishers were apparently clueless about their predicament until the "mad as hornets" Twelfth Wisconsin emerged from the swamps. In their rear, the rest of the First Brigade made a beeline for Orangeburg while the Second Brigade moved on the railroad two miles to the east. Surprised and stunned, the Southerners opened a scattered, though ineffective, bout of musketry. At the bridge, Rebel gunners wheeled their artillery about to offer a few equally ineffectual shells at the advancing Federal skirmishers. Ahead, men were seen running about in confusion at the breastworks, and the whistles of steam engines sounded in

The swamps near the Seventeenth Corps's flanking site at Orangeburg. *Courtesy of the author.*

Orangeburg.[249] The sights and sounds were obvious: the Confederates were abandoning town.

The line collapsing, the Rebels still fighting began falling back through an open meadow toward town. Their Yankee counterparts easily kept them moving rearward, following them over a high sand bank and into the town itself. There the cat-and-mouse game reached an even more feverish pitch. Stevenson's defenders were fleeing, and a train of cars remained behind to help them leave town.

Being Sunday, one family had just returned home from church when the "pitiful" column of retreating Confederates tramped past. The retiring Confederates were halfway to the waiting cars before Yankee skirmishers struck Middleton Street and began firing into their column.[250] Catching a glimpse of their foe's only means of escape only encouraged the pursuing Federals in their zeal. One Yankee recounted the men yelling like Comanches as they chased Confederates down Orangeburg's streets.[251] The fight at Orangeburg was no longer any contest, as the Rebels now wanted nothing more than escaping capture.

Hasty flight was not limited to Stevenson's defenders. The Federal pursuit caught up with Orangeburg's Methodist minister as he returned from church. Trotting down Russell Street, the man of God had eternity in mind as Federal balls flew around him. Putting the whip to his horse, the clergyman hurriedly thundered down the street and turned into his yard unharmed. Fortunately, he would have many more sermons to come.[252]

The tumult was not lost on other inhabitants. Looking down at the festivities, a gaggle of women watched from a balcony as the hooting and hollering Yankees chased their prey. One of the ladies, for whom spunk was obviously not a deficiency, shook her fist in a fit of rage. Not missing a beat, the pursuers shouted, "You dear darlings, where are those fellows of yours. We want to see them." Her Southern blood boiling at the slur on Southern manhood, the young lass's eyes flashed as she called out, "You'll find them! You'll find them, you will! They are waiting for you and they'll make you sorry you ever came into this state! You'll find them, yes, you'll find them, and sooner than you want to!"

The Rebel retreat to the trains, which a biased witness described as being as if "their watches had been a little slow and they were afraid they were behind time," ended with most of the Rebels piling into waiting cars. As these last defenders rode away, Yankee fire ripped into the packed cars. Orangeburg was now officially in Federal hands.[253] An immediate consolation in the prey escaping was found in the depot, as the men found stockpiles of peanuts that were quickly shoved into the victors' haversacks. That night, the captors of Orangeburg ate their gainfully acquired peanuts with great "zeal and animation."[254] Surveying the abandoned fortifications, Oscar Jackson noted sarcastically that the "Chivalry" had run in "total disregard of the South Carolina determination to do or die we have heard so much about."[255]

Forty miles to the northwest, young Emma LeConte recorded the news from Orangeburg with dread: "First and worst, the Yankees are skirmishing at Orangeburg."[256] Deep down, the Southern lass knew that Orangeburg's capture meant no town now stood between Sherman's army and her home in Columbia. Yankees agreed, marching down Orangeburg's streets to the chant of "On to Columbia!" For Orangeburg, their terror was in the here and now. And with its defenders either prisoners or fleeing to Columbia, the town could serve as a preview of what awaited Columbia—now mere days away.

The town's most terrifying hours began. According to Federals, E. Ezekiel—angered by Rebels firing his cotton—set fire in the upper floor of his store at the corner of Russell and Middleton Streets. Before leaving town, the store owner locked the building up tight. Filled with rosin, liquor and other combustibles, the store went up like a pyre. Another Federal version was that the same Jewish proprietor threatened to fire his store should Sherman's men take the town. Whatever role the "curse cotton" played in the conflagration, the remaining bales were committed to the torch.[257]

The rosy image offered by the Federal officers bears a striking contrast with a comrade's testimony. Colonel Oscar L. Jackson recalled the burning of Orangeburg quite differently. According to Jackson, the Federals did just as much to aid the fires as stop them.[258] Of course, local inhabitants concurred with Jackson's claims.

Regardless of their origin, the flames broke through the roof of the store, sending their embers into the stiff gale of wind whipping through the town. Across the street, the store of Chase and Bull erupted into flames, taking the Confederate post office with it. The high winds proved a disastrous element in the mix as the fire spread. Surrounding sheds and quarters helped feed the flames jumping from each closely situated building to the next. As the fire raged, all the stores, businesses and several residences on Russell Street fell victim to the flames.[259]

The flames produced terror wherever they went. While Union soldiers patrolled the streets, a young woman came forward in tears and wringing her hands. Fearful that the fires would soon spread to the house where her grandmother lay ill, she pleaded with the occupiers for aid. To his credit, an officer assured the young lady he would help in her case.[260] Other requests were not as readily acted upon. As Howard entered the flaming town, his efforts immediately went to directing men to follow up retreating Confederates and extinguishing the fires. In the midst of the chaos, a lady approached him requesting a guard over her home. With far too many "irons in the fire," Howard was less than receptive to her request. Insulted, the lady left "deeply vexed."[261] They would meet again.

In only two hours, as much as one-third to half of Orangeburg was in flames. The "grand and beautiful fire" burned throughout the evening despite the efforts of Federals to extinguish the flames.[262] In a testament to the hellish moments of Federal occupation, one unfortunate Union soldier made the mistake of passing a street lined with burning homes. Before he could pass through, a hand and one side of his face were burned.[263]

The human cost in the fight for Orangeburg had also been significant. Three Federals had been wounded, a man of the Sixty-eighth Ohio, Twentieth Ohio and the Ninth Illinois Mounted Infantry. The Rebel cost had been far heavier. Six Rebels were killed, fourteen wounded and twenty-six captured. Twenty of the captives had been among the unfortunates unable to escape the Yankee rush through Orangeburg that Sunday morning.

The entire Seventeenth Corps was in Orangeburg by 4:00 p.m. As the occupiers spread throughout town, the characteristic malevolent occupation began. One family recalled the scene as a Federal officer entered their home, immediately enquiring about "Rebels." With bravery that bordered on foolhardy, the family's matriarch responded, "We are all Rebels." Immediately, the Yankee turned and emptied a bureau of its contents, taking what suited his fancy before leaving. He was merely the first of many as Union officers flooded the home, causing a "terrible day and night" for the "Rebel" family.[264]

Although similar instances doubtlessly occurred, the occupation of the home of Judge Thomas Worth Glover was the most fascinating. Built in 1846, the Glover home was by one recollection the "most pretentious" in town. Spaciousness was hardly a problem, as the home contained eight large rooms, a conservatory and several attic rooms. A Gothic library on the grounds contained the judge's valuable collection. The backyard and grounds captured Glover's prosperity with its large kitchen, laundry rooms and servants' quarters.

It was perhaps such opulence that Sherman's aide de camp, George Ward Nichols, looked upon when he penned, "Tonight we are encamped upon the place of one of South Carolina's most High-Blooded chivalry."[265] Sherman chose the Glover home, opulence and all, to be his headquarters. Ironically, Glover was one of four members of the Secession Convention from Orangeburg. Perhaps this fact was the impetus behind Nichols's scathing slur.[266]

The home's dining room had already been set for dinner when Federal troops helped themselves, scooping up the silverware. In the yard, the library was pillaged while Glover's son-in-law's furniture was piled and burned. By the end of the occupation, Glover's outbuildings were given to the flames while hungry Yankees beheaded his fowls. But the lasting effect of Sherman's army would be the most troubling. One of the Glover sons had already been killed at Second Manassas. Another, Second Lieutenant Leslie Glover, would die a month later against Sherman's army at Averasboro, North Carolina.

Inside the home, Sherman, Howard and others were conferring when Mrs. Glover was brought in. Being Glover's second wife, the former Miss Louisa Carrere of Charleston was found to have history with Sherman. Remembering Sherman from his time as a young U.S. Army officer at Fort Moultrie before the war, Mrs. Glover told him she had seen him act

The Glover home, Sherman's headquarters in Orangeburg. *Courtesy of the author.*

like a gentleman before. Boldly, the lady then informed Sherman that she expected him to behave like one now.[267] Continuing to flatter as if her property's existence depended upon it, Mrs. Glover went on to recite mutual acquaintances that she and Sherman shared. If he had forgotten before, Sherman's own history in Charleston must have come to mind on this trip down memory lane.

Testing his chivalry, Mrs. Glover immediately lodged a complaint with Sherman over an officer who treated her with "marked discourtesy and roughness." Perhaps all but Howard were surprised when she identified the Right Wing commander as the culprit. Mrs. Glover had been the same lady who had unsuccessfully harangued Howard for protection earlier that day. After an explanation in his defense, Howard did make amends by having already sent a guard to look after her home.[268] It is worthy to note the home survived the occupation.

There were other instances of humor and humanity around town. A bored Yankee soldier could not resist sneaking into the newly captured courthouse. His plundering came across a large Confederate flag. Proud of his find, the flag was soon dangling upside down from an upper window of the building. Fortunately for the curious lad, his foray did not occur the following morning. On that occasion, whisks of smoke emerging from the building's roof brought quite the consternation among the local citizens. The source of the ruckus: a rumor that an artillery shell was in one of the upper rooms. As the roof broke out into a blaze, the Yankees milling around town paid no heed to the warnings. A familiar "bang" soon erupted in the building sending showers of hot bricks and debris into the air. Apparently, this is one case where one can believe rumors.[269]

Such levity should not distract us from instances of tragic humanity. Over two hundred children resided in an orphanage in town. As chaos reigned in the streets around them, the children and their Northern caretaker continued with the mundane, singing songs and hymns in a "most credible manner." Of particular "thrilling" effect was one beginning with the poignant, if inapt, words, "I want to be an angel."[270] With the country ravaged and railroads cut all about, the caretaker could only see starvation in the future for her unfortunate charges.[271] As various war-hardened Yankees toured the asylum, quite a few found it quite difficult to maintain dry eyes. Sherman left protection for the asylum from his rambunctious soldiers.[272]

The next day revealed the extent of the collateral costs. The churches and about fifty dwellings were all that remained when Federal troops left town. It was perhaps pragmatism that spared the churches, as the Lutheran church was used as a smallpox hospital, its pews being conscripted into coffins. The Methodist and Presbyterian churches also saw utilitarian use, as their basements became stables for the occupiers.[273] Even such demeaning treatment was better than the alternative since much of the remainder of town was left behind only as "heaps of ashes." One Federal correspondent described the sad sight of the "smoking ruins of the town, the tall black chimneys looking upon it like funeral mutes, and to see old women and children, hopeless, helpless, almost frenzied, wandering amid the desolation."[274] The "pretty village" of Orangeburg lay in ruins. If Orangeburg's fate was any indication, Miss LeConte's anxiety was well founded.[275]

The crossing of the North Edisto was not merely a Seventeenth Corps enterprise. If we recall, we left the Fifteenth Corps at Holman's Bridge on the South Edisto River. On February 11, Logan began his movement on the North Edisto with Hazen's division in the lead. By nightfall, the corps arrived unopposed at former summer resort Poplar Springs after a fifteen-mile march. Bringing up their rear was Corse's division. The Fifteenth Corps was finally reunited.

The Men of This Army Surprise Me Every Day

Poplar Springs owed its moniker to the beautiful poplars that shaded its resident spring. For most of the first half of the nineteenth century, a school flourished on the site. None other than Judge Glover once served as one of its instructors. The resort village once home to both weary refugees from the Lowcountry and young scholars now drew a new group of squatters. [276]

The Fifteenth Corps reunion was not good news for area citizens. Along the North Edisto was the plantation of "Captain Jennings." Now lying unprotected, the plantation was ravaged. One correspondent recalled splendid furniture broken up, a fine library scattered, outbuildings and fences in flames. Picked clean of all provisions, the plantation's mistress was seen boiling leftover corn to feed her children. In illuminating words, our witness claimed to have never witnessed such destruction.[277]

The reunion was also bad news for Brigadier General Joseph Palmer. Palmer's brigade manned the earthworks guarding Shilling's Bridge, the nearby crossing of the North Edisto. Ironically, the hard-luck commander was an antebellum devout Unionist while serving in the Tennessee legislature and as mayor of Murfreesboro. Captured at Fort Donelson, later exchanged and wounded a stunning five times, Palmer now found himself as all that stood between Logan crossing the North Edisto.[278]

Not surprisingly, these troubling days were not the first time that Palmer found himself in Logan's path. Less than a week earlier, Palmer's men fought two separate Yankee probes at Cannon's Bridge. This time the thousands of Federal rifles at Poplar Springs promised an inevitable collision with Palmer's command of fewer than six hundred men. Regardless of his limitations, Palmer was a game officer, stretching his pickets along the river's swamps for over three miles. The main body was concentrated in rifle pits at the bridge itself. At the very least, his men should have warning when the Federals crossed. What he would—or, more accurately, could—do with them once they crossed was another question.

As the sounds of fighting at Orangeburg drifted his way on February 11, Palmer received his own prelude to the trouble to come. Upon reaching Poplar Springs, Logan sent his mounted infantry Palmer's way. Predictably, the bridge burst into flames on sight of Yankees just after Rebel pickets fled across the river. The next morning, Hazen threw his division forward to force the passage. Out front, the 111th Illinois and 53rd Ohio probed toward the bridge. Moving through a waist-deep, half-mile-wide swamp, Yankees sought out whatever lay ahead.

At the bridge, Hazen's skirmishers found it. Across the river, Confederate musketry erupted, drawing Hazen's men into a half-submerged firefight.

Conqueror of the North Edisto: Major General William Hazen. *Courtesy of the Library of Congress.*

A river between them, the continuous fire pinned both sides in place. For the Rebels, their defense was offering a decisive check. Federal attempts to construct rafts were hampered as rifle fire from the north bank kept construction parties dodging unseen tormenters. While skirmishing intensified, the apparent check masked operations that threatened both flanks of Palmer's hapless defenders. The balance of Hazen's division was at work finding a way around the "severe" skirmish developing at the bridge.

If Palmer expected a straight-up fight, he would be sadly mistaken. Hazen slid Colonel Wells Jones's Second Brigade three-quarters of a mile above the bridge. With the other two brigades, Hazen moved a mile and a half below the bridge. Here the river was crossed via the usual aid of fallen timber and hastily constructed rafts. Like comrades all along the river, the downstream flanking party sunk to their waists in the extensive swamp, which stretched for over three-quarters of a mile. Fortunately for the bogged-down Yankees below the bridge, the Second Brigade was having success crossing the river on fallen trees upstream. Battling collective difficulties, Hazen's command struggled slowly through the tangled, swampy morass.

Jones's crossing above the bridge faced the same watery Confederate ally. Over a mile and a half of swamp bordered the river on both sides. This three-layer natural moat kept most of the men wading the waist-deep swamps for several hours as they desperately tried to find the Rebel right flank. The swamp-wading fever must have been contagious, as some envious foragers even waded into the mix just for the "devilment."[279] It seemed that all of Sherman's forces caught the amphibian bug.

By 2:30 that afternoon, the Rebels' sharp defense had kept Logan's corps backed up most of the day. But time had run out for Palmer's riflemen. Suddenly, Yankees emerged from the swamps and struck the right rear of Palmer's line. The stunned Confederates broke. Abandoning their works, they cut free as best they could. Some—overwhelmed by a sense of security offered by unhampered flight— threw away rifles and accoutrements as they ran. The remainder of Hazen's division downstream finally crossed the swamp and struck the Orangeburg and Columbia Road four miles away. Hazen's division had defeated an outnumbered Confederate brigade, but their greatest victory was over the North Edisto.

However surprising the Yankee willingness to wade the swamps was, it did not require Confederate opposition. An Illinois soldier recounted amusingly post-skirmish shenanigans: "It is freezing now and has been very cold all day, yet to get clear water for dinner hundreds of men waded out to the middle of the pond (muddy on the border) over their knees in water. They think nothing of it." The impressed Federal closed the telling anecdote with, "The men of this army surprise me every day with their endurance, spirit, and recklessness."[280] One need not be an admiring comrade to be amazed how rapidly the "amphibious" Federals continued to outflank entrenched Confederates.

Cut off by their comrades' rapid retreat, isolated Rebel pickets were scooped up by the victors. Incidentally, it was the prospect of spending a freezing night in the swamps that convinced one party to surrender. Confederate soldier H.C. Murphy and comrades lay in the swamps for six hours while the fight raged. After the Yankee campfires began to weary the ill-fated Southerners, Murphy understandably broke. Surrendering to the elements as much as Yankees, Murphy "told the boys I could not stand it any longer as I was almost frozen, so we got out of the water and surrendered." Fortunately, they were not alone, as they found a few comrades already as prisoners. Adding insult to injury, on a night called the "coldest of the campaign," the captured Rebels marched in wet clothes.[281]

In all, three Rebels lay dead. Another eighty prisoners were rounded up in the Federal dragnet. In testament to the Confederates' desperate flight, two hundred rifles were captured as spoils. The fighting had killed one and wounded four others of the Fifty-third Ohio while leaving a man from another regiment wounded. An hour before midnight, Jones's victorious Second Brigade, with freezing prisoners in tow, rejoined the division on the Orangeburg Road. The rest of the corps was not far behind. Amphibians to a man, the entire Right Wing had now forced the North Edisto.[282]

Chapter 17

A Conqueror through the Streets of Columbia

Unfortunately swamp fighting lay ahead for the Twentieth Corps as it found one of its most costly days since Savannah at the North Edisto. When we last visited Williams's corps, they lay thawing between the North and South Edisto near Guingard's Bridge. At 2:00 p.m. on February 12, Geary's Second Division reached the North Edisto at Jeffcoat's Bridge. The physical march had been a rough one, particularly for the wagon trains. With the road turned to mush, the men often found themselves pushing out wagons by hand after wheels sank to their hubs.[283] It would be after midnight before the exhausted men laid out blankets and slept.

Brushing aside a detachment of Rebel horsemen, yet another destroyed bridge was found at the end of the familiar causeway. If Geary's men became creative, briers, vines and underbrush covered the swamps bordering the causeway. A more perilous obstacle lay in a barricade manned by an unknown body of Rebels posted across the river. The former military governor of conquered Savannah, Georgia, Geary shook out Brigadier General Ario Pardee's First Brigade to remove them.[284]

Pardee in turn threw forward two companies each from the 5th Ohio and 147th Pennsylvania on either side of the causeway. Amid the tangled swamp, Pardee's skirmishers crept forward. Well shielded, Rebel pickets drew a bead and opened fire, frustrating Yankee efforts to try and cross the rapid-moving, sixty-foot-wide river. As Yankee fire surged, the barricade and river were not protection enough. The Yankees concentrated enough fire to flush the Confederates from the barricade and back up the causeway. To keep

The return of the prodigal son: Brigadier General John Geary. *Courtesy of the Library of Congress.*

Rebels from returning, a company of the 5th Ohio constructed a hasty rifle pit commanding the open causeway. Well covered, the reticent Southerners kept their distance.

The lull did bring to light the greater issue at hand, rebuilding the bridge. For this to happen, the pesky Rebels would have to be dispatched. Toward this end, two companies of the Fifth Ohio were ferried across the river via a small two-man boat. After about twenty men crossed by this tedious process, enough seemed on hand to remove the Rebels. Surely one rush should drive off the dozen Rebels stubbornly staying around. Led by their regiment's colonel, the Ohioans rushed up the causeway. The bold charge initially swept up the road without a single hint of opposition. However, as they nearly reached the far end of the causeway, eardrum-shattering artillery boomed and smoke erupted ahead. The deception became clear: the Rebels were playing the part of ringers. Something more was up the causeway.

Ahead, two concealed artillery pieces completely commanded the causeway. Their deadly fire downed onrushing Yankees, while all those able retreated to the abandoned barricade. Moving to protect his terribly exposed men across the river, Pardee moved three companies of the 147th Pennsylvania into the newly constructed rifle pits. The swamp across the river concealed Deas's brigade, with a section of Kanapaux's artillery. Fortunately for the Federals, the heavy swamp did not provide a strong position from which Deas could harass their work with his 277 rifles. However, Kanapaux's crew used their debut as a deadly opportunity to shell the stymied Federals. While men of the 28th Pennsylvania worked on the bridge and causeway, the South Carolinians sent shell and piercing grape shot to turn the routine work dangerous. The inevitable came as lead from one of the projectiles killed Private Francis Ridgeway while another wounded the regiment's colonel in the foot. Other skirmishing through the day killed enlisted man Jack Rape of the 29th Ohio.[285]

The deadly fire had its desired effect, and work on the bridge was suspended until nightfall. Fortunately for the isolated detachment across the river, the darkness brought about no effort to overrun them. With the threat gone, the First Michigan Engineers were put to work throughout the night repairing the bridge. For at least a time, the work was not without the resumption of Confederate artillery fire. Rebel shots and shells still fell among the engineers, with one shot ripping through the waist of their commander's coat.[286] Despite near misses, the work carried on as the fire slackened.

An hour before midnight, two companies of the 147th Pennsylvania crossed the bridge. Their beleaguered neighbors of the 5th Ohio, who had spent hours crammed behind their fortuitous protector, probably enjoyed their well-overdue relief party. Two hours later, skirmishers discovered the Confederates were long gone, withdrawing in the night. By daylight, Geary's entire division was across the river, skirmishers of the 147th Pennsylvania clearing the way. After a quarter of a mile, Rebels were found again entrenched across a millstream. True to form, the bridge was no more.

Temporarily checked, the Pennsylvanians recovered, shoving the Rebels from the scene. However, Rebel troopers did wound a skirmisher and killed a man of the Fifth Ohio before withdrawing. Geary's command seized the junction of the Edgefield and Orangeburg Road with the Columbia Road. A small party of Rebels, manning a small earthwork, once again offered desultory resistance. However, they were easily dispatched, and Geary halted. His men could finally eat their breakfast.

The fight at Jeffcoat's Bridge had been light by army standards, but the casualties were relatively heavy. Three Federals lay dead, with ten more wounded. At least five of the wounded came from the heavily engaged Fifth Ohio. The Twenty-ninth Ohio had one killed and three wounded, while the Twenty-eighth Pennsylvania had one dead and another wounded. Considering the opposition, it was a stiff price to pay. Despite the blood and toil expended, the remainder of the Twentieth Corps crossed the river throughout February 13 and bivouacked six miles up Columbia Road.[287]

For some, the fight was not over. A foraging party of the Seventieth Indiana made the mistake of venturing too far beyond their own lines. Gobbled up by Rebels, seven men were wounded and captured while some of the survivors returned with all the signs of a hasty withdrawal. Hats, guns, accoutrements, horses and mules were all left behind as casualties to their mad dash for safety. Eager to avenge their unit's honor, the entire regiment marched out only to find the Rebels had slipped away.[288] Such encounters were hardly unusual. "Seldom a day passed," claimed one Union account, that Confederate cavalry didn't clash with Federal foragers.[289]

Foraging efforts were not all calamitous. Some even took on a degree of levity depending on one's perspective. A man of the Eighty-fifth Indiana recalled the humorous scene of an officer "dancing a tune" on the keys of a fine piano. The mansion that contained the impromptu dance floor was shortly engulfed in flames.[290] It was not alone. Littering the countryside were the houses of planters. Almost all had committed the sin of being deserted by their owners. As such, black smoke continued to climb into the sky at all points of the compass. In a retort filled with dark humor, one marauder speculated that building materials would be in high demand in South Carolina after the war.[291]

Revelries aside, the march beyond the North Edisto took on a much more promising hue for foragers and inevitably their hungry comrades. As the ground rose, forage became far more abundant.[292] Every day foragers brought in much of the old staples of their time in Georgia. Turkeys, geese, ducks, chickens, ham, potatoes and honey were among the pleasant surprises. In the words of one beneficiary, "the men were on a quarter rations…and South Carolina had to make up the balance."[293]

The final two ingredients to passage of the North Edisto are the Fourteenth Corps under the controversial Davis and Kilpatrick's cavalry division. Although both would strike the North Edisto around the same time, the adventures of Kilpatrick's troopers along the railroad likely made a few of his troopers more than happy to pass its black waters. After striking Windsor without opposition, Kilpatrick's troopers inflicted the usual damage, destroying several culverts, a water tank, three flat railroad cars and the depot.

Kilpatrick's feign on Augusta would climax with some of his warriors in a race for their lives in a sleepy little town called Aiken. Fittingly, the town's modern incarnation would eventually become known as a center of thoroughbred horse racing. The locally famous "Battle of Aiken" saw the only victory by Confederates on the march to Columbia. The open fighting there saw an early morning attempt by Atkins's Second Brigade to take Aiken end in defeat. For four miles Atkins was driven back to Federal barricades outside town. Much out of character with the swamp fighting we have undertaken to study and being well documented by other fine publications, the clash at Aiken is beyond our scope. Therefore, we will rejoin the Fourteenth Corps and Kilpatrick's move to the North Edisto.

We last left the Fourteenth Corps at Barnwell on February 10. On the two days that followed, Davis's men smashed what was left of the railroad between Williston and Johnson's Station. By February 14, the entire Fourteenth Corps had crossed the South Edisto at Guignard's Bridge, encamping near Dean Swamp. The crossing of the North Edisto over rebuilt Horsey's Bridge went just as smoothly. Two days behind their Right Wing counterparts, the Fourteenth Corps finally conquered the Edistos by nightfall of February 14.[294] Perhaps caught up in the moment, one soldier of the Fifty-second Ohio laconically ended his note on crossing the South Edisto with a boast: "I predict General Sherman will ride, a conqueror through the streets of Columbia, SC."

Other travails, these upon citizens, were also not forgotten. Near Dean Swamp, a division surgeon bearing the iconic name of Doc Watson set out to burn a home. When comrades attempted to "reason" Watson from his incendiary designs, the surgeon issued a threat: "Get out of my way, or I will hit you wiz my schtick."[295] Ironically, the area was no stranger to striving countrymen. Four generations before, Americans fought Americans in a skirmish at nearby Dean Swamp.

Kilpatrick's path would not be so tranquil. Smarting from their severe fight at Aiken, Kilpatrick's division passed the South Edisto easily enough at Guignard's Bridge on February 13. Colonel William Way's dismounted Fourth Brigade had the advance as Kilpatrick marched for Gunter's Bridge the following morning. The march was quiet until reaching the river where the bridge had, as a matter of routine, been burned. Across the river, a detachment of Rebel cavalry held the usual barricade. No matter, Way detached a company from his Second Regiment to plunge into the river and remove the token force.

Throwing their weight around, Lieutenant Oscar Clark's Tenth Wisconsin Battery shelled the post. Meanwhile, the horseless Yankees had their own share of amphibian zeal. Consequently, swamps, a river and barricaded Confederates posed no greater hurdle than the loss of their beasts of war. The river was far narrower than downstream, and the troopers easily swarmed across. Shelled by Clarke's guns and witnessing Yankees pouring out of the swamp, the Rebels abandoned the barricade.

The Yankees had pursued too far, too fast. The Yankee party's flank suddenly exposed, the Confederates moved to drive the audacious Yankees back into the river. Now the pursued, the Yankees fell back to the river to await help. Despite the early reverse, the First Regiment was soon on hand. Superior numbers had once again arrived to undo bold Confederate moves. Overwhelmed, the Rebels retired to a barricaded hill beyond the river. Still smarting from their earlier rebuke, the retired Yankee detachment surged forward again. Swinging wide around to the right, the Yankees suddenly swarmed down on the hill. The resilient defenders—now finding sixty muddied, ornery men charging down on their flank—let loose a single volley before leaving their barricaded perch for good.

All opposition gone, Way crossed over the balance of his brigade and ringed the hill with hearty barricades of his own.[296] The next day, Kilpatrick crossed over the rest of his division, securing the last of Sherman's main columns across the North Edisto River. Any future fights would occur at the virtual gates of Columbia.

Chapter 18

Forests Filled with Flames and Pitch-Black Smoke

With the laurels of his victory over Kilpatrick hanging proudly on the hearts of his redeemed troopers, Wheeler moved on February 12 for Merrit's Bridge over the South Edisto. Sarah Annie Gaston recalled the scene as Wheeler's victorious troops arrived. According to Miss Gaston's recollections, Wheeler's protectors gave more trouble than the Federals. Wasted meat left over from butchered livestock and fires left unattended in the nearby woods kept the family busy for several days. Considering that "Sherman and his marauders" were everywhere, Miss Gaston must have felt she had passed from out of the pan and into the fire.[297] Wheeler was on his way to Columbia.

Meanwhile, Stevenson's corps continued its retreat. Driven from the North Edisto, there was method to Stevenson's madness. As fighting raged at Orangeburg, the Virginian already had clear plans of continuing the fight. From Orangeburg, Stevenson withdrew to the rail depot across the Congaree River at Kingsville. Jackson's and Stovall's brigades took position guarding the valuable railroad crossing of the Congaree. His remaining brigades of Palmer, Deas and Carter retired toward Columbia via their respective roads. Sherman's movement across the North Edisto had also rendered McLaws's defense of the Edisto River at Branchville untenable, sending his division retreating to Four Hole Swamp.[298]

In the midst of the panic, there was a homecoming as Lieutenant General Wade Hampton returned to aid in his home state's defense. Hampton was placed in charge of defending Columbia against Sherman's juggernaut.

For Hampton, the cupboard could scarcely be less bare. With the exception of some militia, Butler's division of cavalry from Virginia and Stevenson's undermanned "corps," the South Carolinian barely had enough to form a strong line of battle. With such forces, Hampton would be tasked with guarding his hometown.

Ignoring the pessimism, Hampton placed Butler's division along the upper fords of Congaree Creek. Stevenson's men held the main bridge over that stream and the fords of the Congaree all the way to the Wateree.[299] Congaree Creek was now very relevant. It was now the first major natural obstacle before Columbia and the last natural line of defense before the Congaree itself. The defense of Congaree Creek kept alive a slim hope. The longer the creek was held, the more time Wheeler and Cheatham's Army of Tennessee corps—coming by way of the Augusta area—had to reach Columbia.

Meanwhile back at Orangeburg, on February 13, the Seventeenth Corps stepped off. Screened by the Ninth Illinois Mounted Infantry, Blair marched his men up the railroad, carefully destroying the track along the way. From Orangeburg to the railroad's intersection with the State Road, Yankees utterly wrecked the line as if they "enjoyed the exercise."[300] Blair's path of destruction was visible for all to see. Columns of smoke from burning buildings, cotton stockpiles and turpentine mills left trails of smoke dotting the horizon. The result was a scene more fit for works of fiction or Old Testament manifestations of the divine as burning pitch fields blacked out the sky with smoke, blocking away the sun. As if carved from a modern war zone, it seemed to a witness as if the smoke of a dozen burning cities overwhelmed both the sky and imaginations of those who witnessed the day's devastation.[301]

Meanwhile, the methodical Federal advance probed toward the Congaree. Lieutenant J.A. McQueen and a small party of scouts moved as far as Fort Motte without incident. Although hard to tell, Fort Motte had its share of history and legend before these tumultuous days. Nearly a century before, famed partisan Francis Marion captured the hamlet's namesake, Rebecca Motte's fortified home via shooting flaming arrows onto her roof. The local heroine had selflessly offered the arrows and her home for the cause of independence. Unfortunately for South Carolinians, heroics of yesteryear would not stop Yankees intent on offering up Carolinian homes to restore the Union.

A historical legacy wasn't the only oddity about the tiny village. A bizarre local legend told of a nocturnal visit by Satan in the mid-eighteenth century. A vivid imagination may have wondered if Rebecca Motte's burnt offering and the satanic tall tale had combined into one frightening saga as Yankee scouts moved threateningly through the village. For the nearby resort village of Totness, hellish destruction had certainly come. The village would not survive the war, reputedly destroyed at the hands of Union soldiers.

At Fort Motte, McQueen learned from local rumors that Rebels were entrenching three miles beyond the railroad bridge to the north.[302] As for the bridge, it was ready for ignition upon appearance of Yankees. By day's end, Blair's corps had destroyed their quarry and pushed two miles northwest of the railroad's intersection with State Road. From Whaley's Plantation, Blair awaited the next day's grand movement. Word from Howard promised more of the old and some new. Blair would detach Force's division to continue destroying the railroad until noon. With the rest of his command, the march would be resumed up State Road to Big Beaver Creek and Sandy Run where the entire corps would eventually rendezvous. Meanwhile, the Ninth Illinois Mounted Infantry would slink up the railroad four miles and destroy the railroad up to the Congaree River. There they would make enough fuss to force any resident Rebels to burn the trestle. If the Confederates didn't cooperate, they would raze the bridge themselves.[303]

The party reached within a few miles of the bridge before the familiar crackle of Rebel musketry greeted them. Pitching in and driving back a band of Rebel cavalry, the bridge was reached easily. There three hundred Confederates had thrown up rifle pits protecting the bridgehead. Dismounting, the Yankees strung out a skirmish line, and the dehorsed troopers had little trouble forcing the roughed-up Rebels to the north bank. Unfortunately for some of the fleeing pickets, the turpentine-laced bridge was ignited before all had retreated safely across. The isolated remnant, faced with the burning trestle to their front and onrushing Federal troopers to their rear, took to the swamps. A couple of men of the Forty-third Georgia were not quite fast enough and were snatched up.

Taking in the scene, the Federals left satisfied that their brief struggle had obtained a practical but superfluous crossing.[304] The rest of the corps had far less amusement, uneventfully reaching Sandy Run post office. Two days beyond Orangeburg, the corps now found itself within a day's march of the outskirts of Columbia. As the men settled in, they would shortly have company. When we last left the Fifteenth Corps, it had just routed Confederates from Shilling's Bridge. The direct Columbia Road, which rose from Orangeburg gently to the northwest toward Sandy Run post office, lay to the east across Caw Caw Swamp just west of Orangeburg. Using the Columbia Road and a plantation road on the west side of Caw Caw, the corps struck out unopposed for Sandy Run.

The scene in the rolling pine country north of the river did have some excitement. One man climbed a tree for a better view of what lay ahead. A cruelly mischievous comrade began chopping at the tree in jest. After the climber failed to heed calls to come down, the chopping eventually sent the pine and its squatter crashing to the ground. An ingloriously injured foot was the reward for the Yankee whose curiosity had painfully gotten the better of his felinelike fun.[305] The "wound" did have one advantage, as the climber earned a wagon ride to recuperate.

Other mischief was far more serious. During one night's march, the surrounding pines erupted into an inferno. The area had once been an orchard where highly flammable pine resin was harvested. Malevolent soldiers, carrying burning pitch on their bayonets, lit the towering pines. As flames ignited dry leaves and resin, the result turned the roadway into one "vast illuminated cathedral, skylit by twinkling stars through its vaulted canopy."[306] The flames crackled throughout, nearly incinerating the men while black smoke choked the roadway.[307]

If they didn't know better, some men may have very well wondered if they were descending into the very depths of hell. In strikingly biblical language, a Union chaplain recalled the impenetrable, awful smoke almost blocking out the sun. Seeing the crackling, raging flames and choking smoke, the minister didn't fail to see the conflagration in hellish terms, recalling, "The scene recalled the vivid pictures of Dante's *Inferno*, Milton's *Paradise Lost*, and the scriptures of Divine truth, illustrative of the punishment prepared for the devil and his angels."[308] Moving beyond theology, the normally verbose George Ward Nichols did not fail posterity when he described the magnificent inferno:

> *Accidentally or otherwise, the dry leaves and pine cones had caught fire, which ignited these trees, and for miles the woods were on fire. It was grand and sometimes awful to see the flames flying over the ground like a frightened steed. As we approached one of these forests, filled with flames and pitch black smoke, it appeared as if we were about to realize the imaginings of childhood, and see dragons and terrible beasts guarding the entrance to some forbidden ground. Wagons, horsemen, and foot-soldiers one by one disappeared into the gloom, to reappear here and there bathed in lurid light. Within, the fire singed our hair and clothes, while our maddened animals dashed hither and thither in an agony of fear. There was a terrible sublimity in this scene which I shall never forget; but is subsequently partook largely of the ridiculous when the column*

went into camp, each man so sooty and begrimed that it was almost impossible to distinguish African from Caucasian.[309]

Surviving their descent into Hades, the corps reached Sandy Run post office by the evening of February 14. Woods's First Division crossed Sandy Run without opposition around 2:00 p.m. and struck out four miles on the Columbia Road. The predetermined camp spot of Wolf's Plantation was reached, and Woods shook out four companies of skirmishers to remove an outpost of Rebel cavalry screening the road. To Woods's rear, the rest of the corps tumbled in.

Woods threw his division into an entrenched line along the hilly terrain. Adding some punch, a battery was slotted into position directly commanding the road. Whatever came their way, Woods appeared ready. Despite the prospect of a long, well-stocked line of freshly piled earth, there was trouble. A band of Rebel cavalry made use of the pitch-black night to swoop down on Woods's advance picket posts. Their sortie captured three men, including the picket line's commander. The short attack was almost certainly a classic "prisoner" snatch, the technique of grabbing prisoners for intelligence.[310] Whatever information was gleaned, the reality was nothing less than grim. The Right Wing was firmly established along State Road.

More bad news was on the way. When we left the men of the Left Wing, its two corps had just crossed the North Edisto at Jeffcoat's Bridge and Horsey's Bridge respectively. Early on February 14, the Twentieth Corps began their march up the direct Columbia Road. The threat of Rebel cavalry hovering on the front and flanks of the column soon reared its ugly head. The outnumbered yet persistent nuisance made little effort to impede Williams's main column. However, loose stragglers and undermanned foraging parties provided a tempting target for sudden Rebel sorties.

Williams's men had no better control over their torches as they too entered the rolling pine country north of the Edisto. A man of the Thirty-third Massachusetts recalled the night sky illuminated and blanketed with smoke for miles around as artificially ignited pines erupted into flames that leapt from tree to tree "swifter than any greyhound." Even a mass of harvested resin was not immune as twenty-five thousand barrels of the fuel was ignited in one grand blaze that rose three hundred feet into the air and produced enough heat to prevent any soul from venturing closer than sixty rods. The smoke reached miles into the air, spreading into what could pass very easily for a dark storm cloud over the land.

In the words of our witness, the region seemed one vast bonfire. More chillingly, he could not help but recall one quip in Savannah shortly before the campaign. Looking across into South Carolina, Sherman allegedly stated, "I will go over there, and what I can't eat I will burn, and I'll make them think hell is coming anyhow." As they watched the conflagration, the Bay State witness surmised that the "South Carolina Chivalry" now probably assumed Sherman's bummers had come from the infernal regions to bring hell home to South Carolina.[311]

Despite such difficulties, the column moved on. By February 15, Williams had his command en route to Lexington in an icy rain shower that mired the column for the second straight day. With the Second Division under Geary leading the way, the column trudged ahead toward Red Bank outside Lexington. Leading the column were the 28th Pennsylvania and a few companies of the 147th Pennsylvania. Almost immediately, Rebel troopers were found. The Pennsylvanians rolled over opposition until coming to Congaree Creek. Here they found about fifty Rebels blocking the crossing from a log breastwork across the stream. With the bridge burned, the four- to five-foot-deep creek offered its own troubles. Surrounding terrain was little better, as a thickly foliaged swamp bordered the creek.

The Federal skirmishers crept up through the swampy thicket. A few hardy souls even managed to cross the creek. With Yankees pressing the bridge and their flank, the Confederates yielded. Yankees bounded across the partially destroyed bridge, replacing its destroyed sections with poles and rails. The impromptu improvements allowed the advance to carry on. Beyond the creek, the fight continued "without intermission." Rebel troopers made use of every ravine and hill to offer a short spurt of opposition.[312] However, Geary's skirmishers kept them moving back to and beyond Red Bank Creek. Flushed back rapidly, this time the Southerners left behind the intact bridge.

Bending but not breaking, the Rebels reined in to make a fight for the Two Notch Road and Columbia Road crossroads two miles from Lexington. Unleashing a deadly volley, the Pennsylvanians broke into a charge. Looking into the face of an onrushing herd of Federals, the Rebels finally broke in confusion. Now having possession of the crossroads, the Yankees' eleven-mile trek placed them only a day's march from the gates of Columbia.

Hearing rumors of Rebel cavalry hovering around, Geary cut the rest and relaxation short for Brigadier General Henry Barnum's 3rd Brigade. The latter was ordered to push on to Lexington. Around 5:00 p.m., Barnum shook out the 137th New York as skirmishers with the guns of the 1st Ohio Light Artillery, Battery C, watching over. The Confederates offered only a few shots before forfeiting the town.

Slightly behind the Twentieth Corps, the Fourteenth Corps did not move from the North Edisto until early February 15. By dark, the Fourteenth Corps joined their comrades near Lexington.[313] Perhaps they heard the sounds of cannons in the direction of the mouth of Congaree Creek. If so, concerned glances looked toward comrades off to their east, while hushed tones circled campfires. Whether they knew or not, the Right Wing had run into something off beyond the pine-timbered horizon.

Chapter 19

The Language Would Create Consternation

Major General John A. Logan must have looked at his battle map with a glimmer of anticipation. As his eyes gazed upon the bisecting lines and names, Columbia loomed largely behind the Congaree River. Early February 15, Congaree Creek sat alone as one more roadblock before Columbia. Rumors circulated that the Rebels held the creek in force, hoping to make its passage a costly one. At 7:00 a.m., Logan's column set off with Charles Woods's division in advance. For Woods, the return to South Carolina must have brought back memories of his visit almost four years before. Leading reinforcements for beleaguered Fort Sumter aboard the *Star of the West*, cadets from the South Carolina Military Academy (now the Citadel) turned back his ill-fated attempt.[314] When Federals spoke of South Carolina as the cradle of the war, Woods could look on with a knowing recollection. Now he found himself marching directly on its capital.

The march to the creek itself should have been an easy one, as only five miles separated it from the Yankee bivouac. Confederates sought to make it a long five miles. Almost immediately, all-too-familiar barricades were found stretched across the road. Behind them were troopers of Colonel William Breckenridge's cavalry brigade. If Woods assumed the Kentuckians would run on sight, he would be sorely mistaken. As Yankees came into view a mile from the Federal bivouac, Breckenridge's troopers opened fire.

Making up the head of the column, Colonel Robert F. Catterson's Second Brigade found itself thrust into action by default. Catterson, earlier charged with building a corduroy able to sustain an army on

A general as "sassy" in battle as politics: Major General John Logan. *Courtesy of the Library of Congress.*

the Salkehatchie, now found himself clearing a path for a corps. Four companies of the Fortieth Illinois sprung forward to clear the way. Caught in the open and less defensible country, Breckenridge's troopers abandoned their barricades, falling back to Savannah Creek before reining in. Shoring up his line, Catterson threw in four more companies of Illinoisans to battle the stubborn Southerners. With Columbia at their back, Confederates seemed far more betrothed to the soil beneath their feet.

The added muscle had its desired effect, and the Southerners were once again clopping away. But the fight had at times broken down into melee. As the "forty men" swarmed over a barricade, one man got tangled up in a "real scuffling fight." Knocking down a Kentuckian, the Yankee afterward choked the Rebel until his surrender.[315] Perhaps the flood of blue overrunning the barricade helped encourage the Southerner's submission.

Though retreating, the stubborn troopers had held up the Yankees for half a day. It wasn't until that afternoon that Federal skirmishers reached the creek. Breckenridge's hard-pressed troopers filed behind a line of fresh rail barricades. Awaiting their arrival was Colonel William McLemore's brigade of Tennessee cavalry. The slight semicircle pattern of the creek allowed the Confederates, under personal command of Brigadier General Dibrell, to extend a tête de pont on the Federal side. Two artillery pieces commanding the road occupied a salient in the barricade.

A cursory glance of the terrain outlying Congaree Creek offered a daunting prospect to the approaching Federals. Flat, open fields extended out beyond the barricades, leaving attackers unprotected from a devastating combination of artillery and musketry. Even the appearance of long, open fields was an illusion. The fields had been forged from the surrounding swampy lowlands. As such, a thick layer of unforgiving mud covered the ground, threatening to further slow attackers.[316] Finally, a couple of brigades of veteran Rebel cavalry, a goodly portion of whom had delayed the Yankees all day, held the position ahead.

As Woods's men came into view, Rebel gunners yanked their lanyards, sending screaming shells toward the emerging Yankees. Catterson's skirmishers crept to within about three hundred yards of the Rebel line before grinding to a halt. One Yankee recalled literally walking into the fighting as he approached the sound of gunfire ahead. Across the field, the smoke and flash of Confederates' weapons were clearly visible. Clearly audible were the whistle of Rebel lead slicing through the air and the thud of exploding shells near the man's now endangered position.[317] He had walked right into a desperate fight for Congaree Creek.

With Rebel artillery and troopers already active behind an unbroken line of barricades, it was now a fight for an entire division. Woods threw Catterson's brigade to the right of the road while Colonel George A. Stone's Third Brigade moved to its left. The First Brigade remained in reserve. Whatever was ahead now had a division coming its way. The plan of action was simple. A line of skirmishers would pin down the Rebels in the barricade. Meanwhile, Stone and Catterson would outflank the Rebel line.

Catterson threw his Forty-sixth Ohio forward; however, Rebel entrenchments across the creek threatened them with a deadly enfilade fire. Fortunately for the sluggish prospects on the Confederate left, Stone's brigade managed to do some jostling on the opposite flank. Stone threw his Fourth Iowa forward as skirmishers fronting two regiments in line. Ahead lay a waist-deep, two-hundred-yard-wide cypress swamp. The Iowans plunged into the swampy morass and swept forward while Rebel musketry and artillery tried their best to bar them from the creek.

The hard soldiering paid off with Stone's men reaching a small branch feeding the creek. More worthy of concern was the discovery of an outpost watching for precisely what they were trying. Three companies of the Fourth Iowa and four companies of the Ninth Iowa easily ran the outpost across the creek. Stone's advance had finally reached Congaree Creek, over five hundred yards above the Confederates' right flank. Wisely, Stone slid the Fourth Iowa three-quarters of a mile upstream beyond the outpost. A lodgment there could roll downstream to block a retreat across the bridge. Unfortunately for Yankees bounding across the creek via a log, alert Rebels sniffed out their foray.

Meanwhile, back in the center, a gun of the First Illinois Light Artillery, Company H, went to work. With the sound of musketry suggesting the swamp on their right had been breached, the defenders soon had even more reason for concern. Taking advantage of Stone's swamp ramblings, the skirmishers in the center rushed forward. Outflanked, their rear in trouble and hard pressed up front, only one thing was left to do: the defenders broke. Dibrell's troopers bailed with the bridge over Congaree Creek in their sights.

As the last troopers cleared the bridge, they piled into an awaiting redoubt. One of the last troopers to cross halted just long enough to light the incendiary-layered bridge, it soon bursting into flames. That the bridge even ignited was a credit to extra preparation, as the continuous rainfall, thick mud covering and soaked timber made igniting the bridge nearly impossible. Luckily, extra flammables in the way of rails helped the saboteur's flame begin its work.

Yankee zeal made the extra effort for not. Seeing the bridge in flames, Lieutenant Colonel Edward N. Upton of the 46th Ohio quickly threw three of his companies forward at the double quick. Firing their weapons on the run, the Ohioans rushed toward the flames. As they reached the bridge, the crash of artillery finally erupted. In a hail of canister, Yankees went to work in kind with their rifles. Although unable to keep Yankees from the bridge, the parting artillery salvos did kill a man of the 100th Indiana. Berated for cowardice, his premonition of death would eerily come to pass.[318]

The Confederates had seen enough and withdrew. Squelching the flames, Yankees had the bridge repaired within minutes. Pursuing the retreating Confederates, Catterson's brigade and the Twelfth Wisconsin Battery, later followed by the balance of Woods's division, crossed and moved about a mile before halting. Shortly after, Hazen's division dropped into bivouac on their right. As darkness crept through the pines, the two Federal divisions went to work, throwing up a line of earthworks from the banks of Congaree Creek to the Congaree River. Beyond their works, Rebel cavalry hovered. It was perhaps fear of Rebel sorties that kept Sherman "nervously pacing back and forth" on the abandoned Rebel works.[319] Sherman's worries were needless. The Federals could sleep easy that night knowing any sortie would run head-on against a steadily improving entrenched line. Not surprisingly, the only mounted threat came as a drunken Confederate colonel strayed too close to the lines.[320]

Although no sober Rebels dashed upon the slumbering Federals, a Rebel battery across the Congaree did keep things lively. Opening an enfilade fire on the distant campfires, the guns harangued Hazen's camp. Little could be done but to suffer through the screaming shells. Some, however, did not remain resigned to their fate. Members of the Fifty-fifth Illinois threw up a traverse keeping the men glued to their earthen protectors the rest of the night. Such precautions did not end the pyrotechnics, as one of the Confederate shells struck a kettle containing a foraged turkey. One Yankee recalled the explosion bringing forth a torrent of profanity that would "cause consternation in a Sabbath school" while leaving little aromatic remnants of the bird or material evidence of the kettle.[321]

The nocturnal barrage took the lives of two and wounded another of Hazen's surprised command. The casualties would be the last of a day that had seen its share. Six Federal soldiers lay dead, while another eighteen were wounded.[322] If our inopportune eyewitness missed the severity of the deadly encounter, it became all too clear as he glimpsed dead from both sides littering the field. One of the lads had the top of his head removed by a deadly projectile that rang true.[323]

Although the passage of Congaree Creek took most of Woods's division, other options were at work to bypass a stubborn Rebel defense. Comfortingly, the Second and Fourth Divisions were on hand throughout the fight should Woods get in over his head. Not to be outdone, their Seventeenth Corps comrades were fast at work upstream at Taylor's Bridge. The Second Brigade of the Third Division was all that was required, and the Sixty-eighth Ohio was moved on the bridge. Slugging through several hundred yards of swamp, the Ohioans finally reached the burned bridge. Its single remaining stringer was crossed, and a Rebel detachment ran off. Giving quite a show, the mud-drenched Federals went to work fortifying while pioneers rebuilt the bridge throughout the night.[324]

Likewise, John Smith's Third Division gave Rebel commanders another concern on the Congaree River six miles below Columbia at Bates Ferry.

Delayed by clogged roads, Smith's column wasn't able to move on the ferry until eleven o'clock that morning. Belatedly reaching his destination, Smith threw out skirmishers of Brigadier General William T. Clark's First Brigade and unlimbered a section of the First Michigan Light Artillery, Company B, to dispatch about thirty Rebel pickets across the river. Unwilling to yield so easily, the Rebels returned fire. It took only a half a dozen shells before the Confederates abandoned their post. Keeping up the deception, Smith spread the Ninety-third Illinois as pickets for over a mile along the river. Little did any lingering Rebels know that the scattered enemy campfires warmed only a Yankee regiment. Their objective accomplished, Smith withdrew to Congaree Creek that night.[325]

Sherman's men were knocking at the gates of Columbia, and their mood reflected it. During the march from Orangeburg, one Hoosier recalled the men breaking loose in a rendition of "John Brown's Body" that reverberated amid the rolling hills. It was fitting that the sectional agitator was spoken of in remembrance as Sherman's army rolled forward toward what should be the last stand of the hated chivalry. If Sherman was to be stopped from taking Columbia, it was now or never.

The Army Marched Triumphantly into Humiliated Columbia

If the spirited defense at Congaree Creek was any indication, Columbia would not fall without a fight. The much larger Congaree River likely lay as the next natural defensive line. With the entire Right Wing now concentrated south of Columbia and the Left Wing moving fast to their west and out of our story, the city found itself as the apex of a great confluence of critical mass.

On February 16, Hazen's division spearheaded the drive on Columbia. Ahead at the Congaree was tough news. Fed by the Saluda and Broad Rivers, the Congaree's wide span would make for a tough crossing. Federal engineers surmised that the best course would be to move farther west and bypass the behemoth Congaree. The Saluda and Broad Rivers offered the option of crossing two smaller rivers rather than one more expansive river.

The drama across the river offered scenes of capitulation. Frantic Confederate authorities were busy evacuating the vast stores from the city before Federal troops overpowered their thin defenses. Perhaps spurred on by the sight of long lines of blue across the Congaree, citizens and squads of Rebel cavalry scurried amid the streets. Some deprived civilians even stopped long enough to raid the railroad depot for sacks of corn and meal.

Overcome with dismay, young Emma LeConte looked at the blue hordes across the river. A few days before, LeConte recorded news of Orangeburg's fall with dread. Miss LeConte now looked at the Yankees filling the outskirts of the city and hauntingly wrote, "Sherman has come, he is knocking at the gate. Oh God! Turn him back! Fight on our side and turn Sherman back!"[326]

As of then, there was no sign of divine intervention. The scene became even more chaotic as a section of Captain Francis De Gress's First Illinois Light Artillery, Battery H, unlimbered on the west end of the Congaree Bridge commanding the main road into the city. Soon shells fell among Confederates racing through the streets. Sherman directed the artillery at the rogue bands raiding supplies and sent a few shots sailing into the unfinished Statehouse walls. The latter targeting was probably used for symbolic effect while the former was to protect the valuable rations.

The arrival of De Gress's battery had been far from routine. Rebel artillery offered instant death to Federals daring to move toward the river. The guns' deadly potential came to fruition by striking down two of Hazen's men.[327] By sections, De Gress ran the gauntlet and began sparring with Rebel counterparts. The addition of the Twelfth Wisconsin Artillery Battery and First Missouri Light Artillery, Company H, increased the pressure on the Rebel guns. In one instance, cheers of triumph sounded as Missouri gunners scattered a Confederate gun crew.[328]

It was not only the Rebel artillery that kept Yankees weary. Rebel sharpshooters were at work. Using a water mill for protection, a nest of Rebels harassed one Federal regiment aligning across the river. After an officer's conspicuous mount drew attention, one volley wounded three Northerners. Several shots from the First Minnesota Battery smashed the wheel into toothpicks, shredding the mill until the Rebels bailed out like "rats from a burning barn."[329] William Fletcher King, who had heard the whistling lead so distinctly at Congaree Creek, watched as suddenly a man crumpled from a Rebel sharpshooter in a spot he had evacuated only minutes before.[330] In response, Federal skirmishers filled the bank with sharpshooters of their own.

The pontoon train had an equally exciting run. A man described the pandemonium as Confederate shells targeted the moving wagons. A riderless horse dashed by, sign of a casualty ahead, while shells exploded overhead. Overshot shells tumbled unexploded along the ground beyond the marching men as providential reminders that the Confederate flag still flew over Columbia. Hastened by the fire, train after train and regiment after regiment passed the gauntlet before the Yankee guns began to make headway. Right Wing commander Howard would later recollect a "pretty hot" time for his men running the sharpshooter and artillery gauntlet before Columbia.[331]

The gallant Confederate gunners and sharpshooters tried, but they were simply outgunned. By day's end, Federal gunners had thrown over 275 rounds into the city and its defenses. However, despite the deadly retort of Logan's artillery, the city of Columbia still held out defiantly. For now, the psychological warfare continued. Flags flew and bands played martial songs, further intimidating Miss LeConte, her neighbors and their protectors. As an obsequious Union soldier had predicted, Sherman was on the verge of marching through Columbia as conqueror.

It was now a matter of finding a way in. With Hazen's division in the lead, the Fifteenth Corps moved to cross the Saluda River at the Saluda Factory a couple of miles to the west. Facing them across the Saluda was, once again, Wheeler's cavalry that had, as usual, torched the bridges.[332] Several hundred yards above the crossing was the yarn- and osnaburg-producing Saluda Factory. The stone-built structure was the source of some disappointment for some of Sherman's "gallant" young staff officers.

With charming recollections of New England factories, the staffers looked forward with "fanciful sketches" to finding a workforce of "pretty, bright-eyed damsels, neatly clad, with a wealth of flowing ringlets and engaging manners." What the crestfallen officers found was quite different. About 250 "unkempt, frowzy, ragged, dirty, all together ignorant and wretched" ladies worked the factory's equally war-wearied equipment. Unlike the witty young soldier at Orangeburg, none of the staffers entertained coming back for any of these Rebel girls.

With the three-hundred-foot bridge gone, the first step in crossing the Saluda would be to secure a lodgment for a pontoon bridge. Their rifles trained on the river, Wheeler's troopers were ready for whatever came. Using bushes and trees for cover, troopers kept up a lively skirmish with Yankees firing from windows of the factory. The "disappointing" workers were at least undeterred by the martial happenings. Running throughout the factory, the ladies frantically tore away as much cloth and yarn as possible to "tote home." Not as repulsed as their officers, some enlisted men took the time to help a few leave with their plunder.[333]

Colonel Theodore Jones's First Brigade drew the duty of clearing away Wheeler's pesky troopers. Loading up in pontoon boats, the Thirtieth Ohio and Fifty-fifth Illinois crossed the river. Landing "in the face" of Rebel fire, the Yankees raced for a rail fence about thirty yards from the river. Rallying into an impromptu line, a signal to move came. Scaling the fence, Hazen's men unleashed both "inspiring cries" and musketry as they charged across the open field. Witnessing the grand charge, one witness recalled never seeing more "spirited, determined fighting than that of those few hundred fellows."[334] Pressed, the Confederates were forced from the woods beyond the river. From their newly won ground on the crest of a ridge, Hazen's advance shielded the Federal work parties enough to complete the pontoon bridge.

The bridge finished, the balance of Jones's brigade crossed and continued the fight. With the Ninth Illinois Mounted Infantry on hand, the reinforced Federals designed to drive remaining Rebels back across the Broad River and save its bridge. With Yankees pursuing closely at the double quick, Wheeler's veterans fell back for two miles, finally fleeing across the bridge over Broad River. Fortunately for Columbia, the Southerners had prepared well. As the retiring Rebels crossed the rosin- and wood-laden bridge, troopers ignited the prized Federal objective. The bridge burst instantly into flames, leaving any attempt to save it in vain. Night's approach made any further attempt to force the Broad River extremely difficult at best. Columbia's defenders had seemingly bought the city at least one more night's freedom.[335]

The "willful" rush for the Broad was as productive as it was rapid. A man of the Fifty-fifth Illinois found himself on a direct beeline for a smokehouse while pursuing retiring Confederates. Without losing a step, the soldier disappeared and emerged from the other side with a ham impaled on his bayonet. A sergeant of the same regiment provided a good example to his men while chasing one particular Confederate trooper. As the Yankee's pursuit got a little too close, the prey ditched his saddlebags full of boiled sweet potatoes and cornbread. In this case, the "loser" of the race gained the leftover spoils as the Rebel escaped.[336]

The difficult crossing aside, Federals on the island between the two rivers had other worries. An accidental fire drove a herd of displaced rattlesnakes straight into the awaiting camps of the 100th Indiana. Luckily, the reptilian invaders bit none of the men.[337] Considering the swamp fighting thus far, it only seemed fitting that South Carolina's reptiles made their own last gasp to stop the Yankees from taking the capital.

Meanwhile, the distant glow of the burning Broad River Bridge troubled Sherman. A pontoon bridge would once again be required. In a campaign of bold river crossings, the Fifteenth Corps was now called on to make the boldest and most important, into Columbia itself. Woods's division would lead the way across the Broad River. If there were any carrots dangled as an incentive for the challenging enterprise, Woods's men would have the distinction of being the first Federal troops to step into Columbia. Now just over four years later, Woods had the opportunity to avenge his rebuke aboard the *Star of the West*.

Stone's brigade would cross first to cover the engineers laying the pontoon bridge.[338] Just like on the Saluda, pontoon boats would ferry Stone's men across. Unfortunately for the Federal officers, who themselves hoped to have troops in Columbia by daylight, the river was far from cooperative.

Come full circle, Brigadier General Charles Woods. *Courtesy of the Library of Congress.*

Lieutenant Colonel William Tweeddale's First Missouri Engineers had the unenviable task of finding a way to get the corps over the river. It would be a task that would prove far more difficult than the casual observer could possibly imagine.

Battling Tweeddale's engineers was the rapid current that moved the already high stream. Modern-day kayakers can well imagine the difficulties as the river churned before the Yankee engineers. Sharp Rebel fire offered its own trouble requiring covering fire from Yankee artillery and musketry.

Complicating matters further was the pitch-black darkness that marred visibility. There was at least some good news as Tweeddale found a location a half a mile above the old bridge and two miles above Columbia.

Before a ferry of pontoon boats could cross the river, a ferry line would have to be placed across the river. As the heavy current raged, repeated attempts to get a line established were for naught. The aggravation continued until a light cord was obtained at the nearby factory. Using the new discovery, a rope ferry was finally laid across around 3:00 a.m. A stable foundation now in place, several boats were soon locked together and planked.[339] The hard work would pay off in the way of a bridge.

Less than an hour later, Stone ferried over two boatloads of skirmishers. Thrown out seventy-five yards from the river, strict orders were issued against firing unless attacked. A complicated nighttime river crossing was even thornier during a premature firefight. Soon after, the Thirty-first Iowa arrived and went to fortifying the newly formed bridgehead. Awaiting the arrival of the balance of his brigade, Stone took the time to get a grasp of his precarious situation. Stone had landed on a small, crescent-shaped swamp masquerading as an island. Lying between the island and firm ground were several twenty-foot-wide bayous filled with waist-deep water. Beyond this natural moat stretched a natural breastwork of tangled underbrush and timber. Shortly thereafter, Rebel gunfire let Stone know his crossing had not gone unnoticed.

Stone had run into old friends. From behind trees and bushes, Palmer's recently "jaded" brigade opened up a hot fire on the blue figures hunkering in the swamp below them. As lead zipped among them, Yankee skirmishers were probably glad they had taken the time to fortify their suddenly hot position. Virtually alone, Stone soon became aware of even more frightening developments, as the Confederates seemed to be gaining strength toward their own right flank. With reinforcements being shifted against his left, the Rebels may soon be able to pin Stone down with enough force that he would be hard pressed to fight his way through.

With his entire brigade on hand by 7:00 a.m., Stone had a decision to make. The time for prudence had passed, as too much had already been accomplished to be cautious now. Sensing the climactic moment was at hand, Stone determined to run his men through whatever lay ahead. It was time for one more "Sherman battle in miniature." The Thirty-first Iowa was aligned facing the Rebel right flank. The Ninth Iowa moved even wider to align on their left. On the advance, the Ninth Iowa would swing around at the double quick and take the Rebel line in flank. Meanwhile, the Thirtieth

Iowa would strike directly from the island with the Twenty-fifth Iowa and still arriving Fourth Iowa in reserve. If all worked correctly, the Rebels would be struck simultaneously on both their front and right flank.

Aided by skirmishers and artillery across the river, Stone lunged forward. As the men of the Thirtieth Iowa came upon the submerged ravines, a few waited for the advantage of a fallen tree to cross. Most swarmed both over and through the natural impediment, holding both rifle and cartridge box overhead to protect them from the ruin. Once again, Palmer's brigade found themselves overwhelmed by Yankees suddenly emerging from the swamps. The speed and audacity of the attack caught the stunned Rebels by surprise as thirty were snatched up as prisoners. Once more, at the most important time of all, Sherman's men had become amphibians.

Palmer's men gave up their ground. In fact, Stone's rapid advance threw Palmer and a regiment of Wheeler's cavalry back, only coming to a halt as the desperate Rebels began turning his flank. Wisely, Stone halted and fortified the commanding ridge he had just snatched from his foes. As support arrived, Stone moved on the city. The Rebel troopers screening his front gave ground easily. Arriving within a mile of the city, a carriage approached. Emerging from the carriage was Mayor Goodwin and the alderman of the city. The city had been evacuated, Goodwin claimed, and he had come to surrender the city before any more damage could occur. It seemed two weeks of swamp wading and a morning of fighting had gained Columbia.

Stone, cast in his historic position, would accept nothing less than unconditional surrender of the city. Stone, Major Anderson of the Fourth Iowa and Captain Pratt of Logan's staff joined the carriage ride and headed back into the city with the mayor's entourage. The irony of a "Major Anderson" being one of the first Federal officers to reenter the capital of the state that made Fort Sumter a national icon was perhaps running through the minds of the carriage passengers until trouble stirred just outside town. About fifteen of Stone's skirmishers came tumbling back, driven in by a portion of Wheeler's rear guard. Was Goodwin party to a last-ditch Confederate ruse?

The situation was awkward at best for the mayor. Minutes after the city's supposed surrender, a battalion of Rebel cavalry was pushing back the Federal vanguard. Angered by this possible ruse and the more personal danger should the Rebel detachment get any closer, Stone rounded up forty flankers and rallied his bemused skirmishers. As one last precaution, Stone left a corporal and three men in charge of the mayor and his party. Stone's subsequent orders were chilling. Should any of the Federal skirmishers be wounded or killed, the corporal was to shoot the captives. If this were a Rebel ruse, the mayor and alderman would be casualties as well.

Fortunately for Mayor Goodwin and his entourage, the Rebels had as little marksmanship as pluck. Stone's makeshift detachment dispersed the Rebel threat and entered town. Ahead of comrades, Stone's Iowans and a detachment of the Thirteenth Iowa and Thirty-second Illinois of the Seventeenth Corps raced toward the nearest symbols of state authority. For the first time in four years, the Stars and Stripes was raised over the home of the state's highest office, the Statehouse. The Seventeenth Corps detachment, fresh from crossing the Congaree via a skiff, planted the nation's flag upon the governmental bastions, the old and new capitol buildings.

Two more weeks of campaigning and the burning of Columbia remained to come. But with the United States flag flying once again over Columbia, symbolically South Carolina's conquer had finally come. Columbia's capture represented a month's subjugation of the worst rivers, swamps and creeks South Carolina could offer. Bands of brave Confederates manning formidable positions had been subdued in almost daily conflict. Blackened ruins and chimneys marked miles of punished countryside and towns. Surely, it had taken a special kind of army to accomplish such complete subjugation of South Carolina.

Upon hearing of Sherman's men passing the South Carolina swamps, a wowed enemy proclaimed Sherman's army had no equal since the days of Julius Caesar. But its leader had a different kind of army in mind. In January 1865, Sherman quipped that his men were "not exactly amphibious" yet. Along the swamps of the South Edisto, there was still a degree of doubt as he reasoned that his army must "all turn amphibious, as the country is half under water." But as Yankees marched into Columbia chanting, "Hail Columbia, Happy Land, if I don't burn you I'll be d——d," it became all too clear that the boys of Sherman's army had certainly risen to the challenge.[340] None could doubt now that they were truly an army of amphibians.[341]

Notes

1. WILL THEY INVADE US?—WHERE IS THEIR ARMY?

1. Warner, *Generals in Blue*, 538.
2. OR, Reports, 782, 794, 795–6, 802 3.
3. Gross, 247–8; Fleharty, 130–1.
4. OR, Correspondence, 985.
5. OR, Correspondence, 12–3.
6. Brant, 90–1.
7. Fleharty, 131.
8. Brant, 90–1.
9. Underwood, 258.
10. OR, Correspondence, 15.

2. YOU'D BETTER GET OUT; WE ARE THE FIFTEENTH CORPS

11. Warner, *Generals in Blue*, 36.
12. OR, Reports, 374–5, 1,133, 87; OR, Correspondence 1,010–1.
13. Howard, 101.
14. Warner, *Generals in Gray*, 204–5.
15. OR, Correspondence, 1,015.
16. Howard, 102.

17. OR, Reports, 374–6, 192–3.
18. Warner, *Generals in Blue*, 238.
19. Sherman, 254.
20. OR, Correspondence, 54.
21. Warner, *Generals in Blue*, 459.
22. OR, Reports, 314–6.

3. There Goes Your Old Gospel Shop

23. Warner, *Generals in Blue*, 248.
24. Bull, 202.
25. OR, Reports, 581–2, 597–8.
26. Underwood, 258.
27. McBride, 164.
28. OR, Reports, 782–3, 802–4.
29. Bull, 203.
30. Hicken, 291.
31. Underwood, 258.
32. Osborne, 187; Merrill, 240–1.
33. Fleharty, 132.
34. Bull, 203–4.
35. Bowen, 133; Bryant, 303; Underwood, 259.
36. Bradley, G.S., 250.
37. OR, Correspondence, 148–9.

4. They Are South Carolinians, Not Americans

38. Bryant, 303.
39. Merrill, 241.
40. OR, Reports, 597–9, 635–6, 607–9, 618–21, 659–60.
41. G.S. Bradley, 253.
42. OR, Reports, 655–6.
43. Thomas O. Lawton, 3–6, 8–11.
44. Jones, *When Sherman Came*, 111–2.
45. Marszalek, 321.
46. Lawton, Thomas O., 11–2.
47. Jones, *When Sherman Came*, 48.

48. Nichols, 173.
49. Hurst, 169.
50. Nichols, 194.
51. Stevenson, 139; Byers, 7.
52. Thomas O. Lawton, 11–3.
53. G.S. Bradley, 251.
54. OR, Correspondence, 342.
55. Grimsley, 201.
56. Bull, 207; OR, Reports, 620.
57. OR, Reports, 560–1.
58. Ibid., 607–9, 597–9, 618–21.
59. Ibid., 607–9.
60. OR, Correspondence, 173–4.

5. Here Began a Carnival of Destruction

61. OR, Correspondence, 1,066; OR, Reports, 375–6, 193, 221–2.
62. Warner, *Generals in Blue*, 155.
63. OR, Correspondence, 1,073–4, 1,074, 180–1, 171–2.
64. Howard, 105.
65. Thomas Ward Osborn, 92.
66. Warner, *Generals in Blue*, 338–9.
67. Anders.
68. Johnson, 30.
69. Moore, et al., 380, 386, 420.
70. Wills, 339.
71. Gage, 274–5.
72. Grimsley, 16.
73. OR, Correspondence, 741, 799–800. Letter found in OR vol. 44.
74. Trimble, 166.
75. Gage, 274–5; Wills, 339.
76. OR, Correspondence, 1,075–7, 173, 171–2.
77. Hilton, 83.
78. Gage, 274–5.
79. Swan, 197.
80. Brown, 367.
81. OR, Reports, 251; OR, Correspondence, 196.
82. Wills, 339; Gage, 275–6.

83. Conyngham, 306.
84. OR, Reports, 222.

6. MEN GASPING IN DEATH

85. OR, Reports, 420.
86. OR, Correspondence, 181, 195, 207, 203.
87. Warner, *Generals in Blue*, 225–6.
88. OR, Correspondence, 196.
89. *Proceedings of the Massachusetts Historical Society*, 396.
90. OR, Reports, 289, 222, 272, 81.
91. Conyngham, 306–7, 311; Sligh, 34.
92. OR, Correspondence, 208, 205.
93. Thomas Ward Osborn, 94.
94. Ibid.
95. Williams.
96. Thomas Ward Osborn, 95.
97. Moore.
98. Bell, 36
99. Thomas Ward Osborn, 95.
100. Ibid.
101. Bell, 36.
102. Hays, 69.
103. OR, Correspondence, 286.
104. OR, Correspondence, 1,076. Also an officer on January 31.
105. Bell, 31, 45, 64.
106. Wilson, 411–2.
107. Jackson, 177–8.
108. Bell, 54.
109. Jackson, 177–8.
110. Williams.
111. Moore.
112. Description of Rivers' Bridge from the following: OR, Reports, 193–5, 376–7, 386–90, 400–1, 397–9, 393–4, 411–2.
113. King, 223–4.
114. Williams.
115. Thomas Ward Osborn, 102.
116. OR, Reports, 405–6.

7. Yanks, You Better Leave This Country

117. OR, Correspondence, 1,063, 198, 208, 582.
118. Ibid., 1,075. Likely either Dibrell's or Breckenridge's brigade.
119. Fleharty, 133.
120. Ibid.; Merril, 241; OR, Reports, 582, 782, 788, 796, 798.
121. G.S. Bradley, 255.
122. OR, Reports, 222, 310, 272–3, 89.
123. Brown, 368.
124. OR, Reports, 843, 803.
125. McBride, 165; Gross, 249.
126. Fleharty, 135.
127. G.S. Bradley, 256–7.
128. Lawton and Wilson, 183.
129. McBride, 165.
130. OR, Reports, 857.
131. Thomas O. Lawton, 11.

8. Build Them Strong, Catterson

132. OR, Reports, 222, 194.
133. Brabham, 72–83.
134. Clark, 189–90.
135. OR, Reports, 222.
136. Hitchcock, 255; Nichols, 137–9.
137. Wills, 341.
138. Ibid.
139. Hitchcock, 256.

9. Those Fellows Are Trying to Stop Us

140. OR, Correspondence, 308, 306, 401, 403.
141. Osborn, 105.
142. Ibid.
143. OR, Reports, 408; OR, Correspondence, 309, 318–9.
144. Warner, *Generals in Blue*, 459.

145. OR, Reports, 317.
146. Hitchcock, 259; Wills, 341.
147. Hitchcock, 258.
148. OR, Correspondence, 320; OR, Reports, 317, 222–4.
149. Hitchcock, 259.

10. NOTHING IN SOUTH CAROLINA WAS HELD SACRED

150. Niles, 279.
151. OR, Reports, 383; OR, Correspondence, 310.
152. Underwood, 262.
153. Fleharty, 135.
154. Brant, 96.
155. Underwood, 262.
156. G.S. Bradley, 258.
157. OR, Correspondence, 311–2.
158. Lawton and Wilson, 47–8.
159. OR, Reports, 891, 896, 884.
160. Jones, *When Sherman Came*, 114–5, 121–3, 125.
161. Ibid.
162. Jones, *When Sherman Came*, 121; Hamilton, 178–9.
163. OR, Reports, 858, 878–9, 881, 887, 908.
164. OR, Reports, 858, 864, 865, 872, 874.
165. OR, Correspondence, 406–7.

11. A HASTY VISIT TO MR. SIMMS

166. OR, Correspondence, 1,088.
167. Warner, *Generals in Gray*, 292–3.
168. OR, Correspondence, 1,094, 1,100.
169. Osborn, 105–6.
170. OR, Correspondence, 332; OR, Reports, 195, 224, 245, 252.
171. Conyngham, 307.
172. Osborn, 108.
173. OR, Correspondence, 322; OR, Reports, 195, 412.
174. Osborn, 107.

175. Osborn, 107–8; Pepper, 334.
176. "Operations on the Atlantic Coast," 444–5.
177. Ibid.
178. Conyngham, 319.
179. Simms, 18–9.
180. Conyngham, 319; "Operations on the Atlantic Coast," 446.
181. Nichols, 144.
182. OR, Correspondence, 328, 376.
183. Clarke, 251.
184. OR, Reports, 377; OR, Correspondence, 328, 343, 334.
185. OR, Reports, 224, 279, 297, 308–9.
186. OR, Reports, 583, 128, 647–8; OR, Correspondence, 336, 329.
187. Upson, 123.
188. OR, Correspondence, 333–4, 348–9, 330, 349, 342.
189. Underwood, 262.
190. Brant, 96.
191. OR, Correspondence, 349, 364–5.
192. Underwood, 262.
193. Fleharty, 136.

12. The Plantations Now Looked Desolate

194. OR, Reports, 682–3.
195. Bull, 206–7.
196. Ibid. 208.
197. Ibid.
198. OR, Correspondence, 349–50, 299; OR, Reports, 682–3, 620, 608–9, 756.
199. OR, Reports, 221, 337.
200. Warner, *Generals in Blue*, 94–5.
201. OR, Reports, 335–8, 355; OR, Correspondence, 332.

13. The Most Complete Rout I Have Ever Witnessed

202. OR, Reports, 429–30, 444–5, 550.
203. Girardi, 328; Holmes, 20.

204. Bishop, 171.
205. Calkins, 287.
206. OR, Reports, 858, 891–2, 896, 898–9, 900–1.

14. Only Those Who Were There Could Tell

207. Fleharty, 137.
208. OR, Reports, 224; OR, Correspondence, 358–9, 344.
209. Crooker, 405–6.
210. Warner, *Generals in Blue*, 70.
211. Eddy, 360.
212. OR, Reports, 272, 287; OR, Correspondence, 361.
213. Crooker, 405–6.
214. Barnes, 160. From a letter that Barnes claims to have memorized that was found on Hull.
215. Mark Bradley, 61–2.
216. Anders, 303.
217. Osborn, 112.
218. Anders, 304.
219. Barnes, 155–8.
220. OR, Reports, 195, 377–8, 389–90, 398, 401–2; OR, Correspondence, 359, 360, 362–3.
221. Barnes, 156–9.
222. Hunter, 5.
223. Howard, 109.
224. OR, Reports, 378.

15. As If a Knife Was Cutting the Flesh

225. OR, Correspondence, 1,134–5, 1,128.
226. Ibid., 1,125.
227. Ibid., 378; OR, Reports, 279, 224, 337–8.
228. Bull, 209.
229. Morhouse, 156.
230. OR, Reports, 610, 684, 598.
231. Morhouse, 156–7.
232. Bull, 210.

233. OR, Reports, 782, 381.
234. Fleharty, 137–8.
235. Underwood, 263.
236. Fleharty, 137–8; Underwood, 263; OR, Reports, 782–3, 804, 814, 821–2, 831–2.

16. The Men of This Army Surprise Me Every Day

237. OR, Correspondence, 374–5, 385.
238. Ibid., 380.
239. *Recollections and Remininsces*, Vol. 4, 265–6.
240. Force, 271.
241. Nichols, 339.
242. Wood, 28.
243. Force, 271.
244. Rood, 401
245. *Recollections and Remininsces*, Vol. 4, 265–6.
246. Woods, 28.
247. Rood, 401.
248. Ibid.
249. Morris, 149.
250. Dibble, 11.
251. Rood, 401–3.
252. Dibble, 11.
253. Rood, 401–3.
254. Morris, 149.
255. Jackson, 179–80.
256. LeConte, 29.
257. Rood, 403.
258. Barrett, 58–9.
259. Dibble, 12.
260. Rood, 402.
261. Howard, 111–2.
262. Thomas Ward Osborn, 117–8; Nichols, 149.
263. Rood, 402.
264. Dibble, 13.
265. Nichols, 149.

266. Salley, 38–40.

267. Ibid.

268. Howard, 111–2.

269. Rood, 403.

270. Pepper, 322.

271. Conyngham, 323–4.

272. Calkins, 287.

273. Bennet, 9.

274. Conyngham, 323.

275. OR, Reports, 406–9, 378–9, 196–7.

276. Bennett, 27.

277. King, 224.

278. Warner, *Generals in Gray*, 228.

279. Wills, 345.

280. Ibid.

281. *Recollections and Reminiscences*, Vol. 1, 301; Belknap, 450.

282. OR, Reports, 196, 225–6, 279–80, 297–8, 301–2, 287, 305, 308, 308–10; OR, Correspondence, 385, 386, 398–9.

17. A Conqueror through the Streets of Columbia

283. Bull, 210.

284. Warner, *Generals in Blue*, 169.

285. SeCheverell, 143.

286. Sligh, 36.

287. OR, Reports, 684–5, 705–6, 727–8, 720–1, 715–6, 717, 713, 1,111.

288. Fleharty, 138.

289. Morhouse, 157.

290. Brant, 97.

291. Morhous, 157.

292. Hartwell Osborn, 190.

293. Morhouse, 157.

294. OR, Reports, 430, 550–1.

295. Holmes, 21.

296. OR, Reports, 902–3.

18. FORESTS FILLED WITH FLAMES AND PITCH-BLACK SMOKE

297. *Recollections and Reminiscences*, Vol. 1, 541–2.
298. OR, Correspondence, 1,167, 1,185, 1,094.
299. Ibid., 1,177–8.
300. Howard, 111; OR, Correspondence, 400.
301. Osborn, 119–20.
302. OR, Correspondence, 418; Stoney.
303. OR, Correspondence, 409.
304. OR, Reports, 378–9; Smith, 412; OR, Correspondence, 418, 421.
305. Crooker, 407.
306. King, 225.
307. Wills, 345.
308. Gage, 280–1.
309. Nichols, 153–4.
310. OR, Reports, 225–6, 242.
311. Underwood, 264.
312. Boyle, 280; Gross, 249.
313. OR, Reports, 583, 686, 706–7, 751, 765, 430–1, 446, 479–80, 721.

19. THE LANGUAGE WOULD CREATE CONSTERNATION

314. Warner, *Generals in Blue*, 572.
315. Wills, 350.
316. Nichols, 340.
317. King, 226.
318. Upson, 151.
319. King, 226.
320. Wills, 350.
321. Crooker, 408.
322. OR, Reports, 197–8, 225–6, 242–3, 258, 260–2, 266–7, 271–2, 317–8; OR, Correspondence, 1,213.
323. King, 226.
324. OR, Reports, 379, 407.
325. Ibid., 318, 326; OR, Correspondence, 432.

CONCLUSION: THE ARMY MARCHED TRIUMPHANTLY INTO HUMILIATED COLUMBIA

326. Jones, *Heroines of Dixie*, 360.
327. OR, Reports, 20–1, 271–2.
328. King, 228.
329. Davis, 193.
330. King, 228.
331. Howard, 119; OR, Reports, 298.
332. OR, Reports, 371–3; OR, Correspondence, 1,199.
333. Nichols, 156–9.
334. Ibid.
335. OR, Reports, 379, 287.
336. Crooker, 408.
337. Upson, 152. Although reported as occurring at a later date.
338. OR, Correspondence, 445–6; OR, Reports, 243, 263–4.
339. Osborn, 128.
340. OR, Reports, 379, 412, 417; OR, Correspondence, 457.
341. OR, Correspondence, 104, 365.

Bibliography

Anders, Leslie. *Eighteenth Missouri*. Indianapolis, IN: Bobbs-Merrill, 1968.

Barnes, Henrietta, *Our Women in the War: The Lives They Lived; the Deaths They Died*. Charleston, SC: Post and Courier Press, 1885.

Barrett, John G. *Sherman's March Through the Carolinas*. Chapel Hill: University of North Carolina Press, 1956.

Belknap, William. *History of the Fifteenth Regiment Iowa Volunteer Infantry: From October, 1861 to August, 1865*. Keokuk, IA: R.B. Ogden and Son, 1887.

Bell, Daniel J. *The Strongest Position I Ever Saw in My Life: Mapping and Site Study of the Rivers' Bridge Battlefield*. Columbia: South Carolina State Park Service, 2005.

Bennett, Addie Owen. *Orangeburg 1735*. Orangeburg County Library, Orangeburg, S.C.: 1961.

Bishop, Judson Wade. *The Story of a Regiment: Being a Narrative of the Service of the Second Regiment, Minnesota Veteran Volunteer Infantry*. St. Paul, MN: 1890.

Bowen, James Lorenzo. *Massachusetts in the War, 1861–1865*. Springfield, MA: Clark W. Bryan and Co., 1889.

Boyle, John Richards. *Solder's True: The Story of the One Hundred and Eleventh Regiment, Pennsylvania Veteran Volunteers*. New York: Eaton and Mains, 1903.

Brabham, M.M. *Mizpah: A Family Book Including a Family Sketch of Buford's Bridge and its People*. Columbia, SC: R.L. Bryan Company, 1923.

Bradley, G.S. *The Star Corps, or Notes of an Army Chaplain During Sherman's Famous March to the Sea*. Milwaukee, WI: Jermain and Brightman, 1865.

Bradley, Mark. *Last Stand in the Carolinas: The Battle of Bentonville*. Campbell, CA: Savas Publishing Company, 1996.

Brant, J.E. *History of the Eighty-Fifth Indiana Volunteer Infantry, Its Organization, Campaigns, and Battles*. Bloomington, IN: Cravens Bro., 1902.

Brown, Alonzo. *History of the Fourth Regiment of Minnesota Infantry*. St. Paul, MN: Pioneer Press Company, 1892.

Bryant, Edwin Eustace. *History of the Third Regiment of Wisconsin Veteran Volunteer Infantry*. Madison, WI: Veterans Association of the Regiment, 1891.

Bull, Rice. *Soldiering: The Civil War Diary of Rice C. Bull*. Edited by K. Jack Bauer. New York: Berkely Books, 1977.

Byers, S.H.M. *What I Saw in Dixie or Sixteen Months in Rebel Prisons*. Dansville, NY: Robbins and Poore, 1868.

Calkins, William W. *History of the One Hundred and Fourth Illinois Vol. Infantry in the War of the Great Rebellion, 1862–1865*. Chicago: Donnehue and Henneberry, 1895.

Clarke, Olythus B. *Downing's Civil War Diary (Diary of Sergeant Alexander G. Downing)*. Des Moines: Historical Department of Iowa, 1916.

Clark, Walter. *Histories of the Several Regiments and Battalions From North Carolina in the Great War 1861–1865*. Vol. 3. Goldsboro, NC: Nash Brother Printers, 1901.

Conyngham, David. *Sherman's March Through the South*. New York: Sheldon and Company, 1865.

Crooker, Lucien B. *The Story of the Fifty-Fifth Regiment Illinois Volunteer Infantry in the Civil War*. Clinton, MA: W.J. Coulter, 1887.

Davis, Washington. *Campfire Chats of the Civil War*. Lansing, MI: PA Stone and Company, 1889.

Dibble, Thomas O.S. *History of Orangeburg, 1884*. Orangeburg, SC: Orangeburg County Free Library, 1953.

Eddy, T.M. *The Patriotism of Illinois*. Vol. 2, Chicago: Clarke and Co., 1866.

Fleharty, Stephen F. *Our Regiment: A History of the 102nd Illinois Infantry Volunteers*. Vol. 102, Part 4. Chicago: Brewster and Hanscom, 1865.

Force, Manning F. *General Sherman*. New York: D. Appleton and Company, 1899.

Gage, Moses D. *From Vicksburg to Raleigh or a Complete History of the Twelfth Regiment Indiana Volunteer Infantry*. Chicago: Clarke and Co., 1865.

Girardi, Robert. *Campaigning with Uncle Billy: The Civil War Memoirs of Sgt. Lyman S. Widney*. Victoria, BC: Trafford Publishing, 2008.

Grimsley, Mark. *The Hard Hand of War: Union Military Policy Toward Southern Civilians, 1861–1865*. Cambridge, NY: Cambridge University Press, 1995.

Gross, Lewis M. *Past and Present of DeKalb County, Illinois*. Volume 1. Chicago: Pioneer Publishing, 1907.

Hamilton, William Douglas. *Recollections of a Cavalryman in the Civil War after Fifty Years, 1861–1865.* Columbus, OH: F.J. Heer Printing Co., 1915.

Hays, E.Z. History *of the Thirty-second Regiment: Ohio Veteran Volunteer Infantry.* Columbus, OH: Cott and Evans Printers, 1896

Hicken, Victor. *Illinois in the Civil War.* Champaign: University of Illinois Press, 1991.

Hilton, Mary Kendall. *Old Homes and Churches of Beaufort County.* Columbia, SC: State Printing Company, 1970.

Hitchcock, Henry. *Marching with Sherman, Passages from the Letters and Campaign Diaries of Henry Hitchcock.* New Haven, CT: Yale University Press, 1927.

Holmes, J.T. *Then and Now.* Columbus, OH: Berlin Printing Company, 1898.

Howard, Oliver Otis. *Autobiography of Oliver Otis Howard, Major General U.S. Army.* Vol. 2. New York: Baker and Taylor Company, 1908.

Hunter, Robert. *Sketches of War History, 1861–1865: Papers Read Before the Ohio Commandery of the Military Order of the Loyal Legion of the United States.* Vol. 1. Cincinnati, OH: R. Clark and Co., 1888.

Hurst, Samuel H. *Journal History of the Seventy-Third Ohio Volunteer Infantry.* Chilicothe, OH: 1866.

Jackson, Oscar L. *The Colonel's Diary. Journals Kept Before and During the Civil War by the Late Colonel Oscar L. Jackson...Sometime Commander of the 63rd Regiment O.V.I.* Sharon, PA: 1922.

Johnson, Thomas Cary. *The Life and Letters of Benjamin Morgan Palmer.* Richmond, VA: Presbyterian Committee of Publication, 1906.

Jones, Katharine M. *Heroines of Dixie: Confederate Women Tell Their Story of the War.* Westport, CT: Greenwood Press, 1973.

———. *When Sherman Came: Southern Women and the Great March.* Indianapolis, IN: Bobbs-Merrill Company, Inc., 1964.

King, William Fletcher. *Reminiscences.* New York: Abingdon Press, 1915.

Lawton, Alexania E., and Reeves Wilson. *Allendale on the Savannah.* Bamberg, SC: Bamberg Herald Printers, 1970.

Lawton, Thomas O. *Upper St. Peter's Parish and Environs.* Garnett, SC: Thomas O. Lawton Books, 2001.

LeConte, Emma. *When the World Ended: The Diary of Emma LeConte.* Lincoln: University of Nebraska Press, 1987.

Marszalek, John F. *Sherman: A Soldier's Passion for Order.* New York: Free Press, 1993.

McBride, John Randolf. *History of the Thirty-Third Indiana Veteran Volunteer Infantry.* Volume 33, Part 4. Indianapolis, IN: W.M. Burford, Printer and Binder, 1900.

Merrill, Samuel. *The Seventieth Indiana Volunteer Infantry in the War of the Rebellion.* Indianapolis, IN: Bowen-Merrill Company, 1938.

Moore, Alexander, George Rodgers and Lawrence S. Rowland. *The History of Beaufort County, South Carolina*. Columbia: University of South Carolina Press, 1996.

Morhouse, Henry C. *Reminisces of the One Hundred and Twenty-Third N.Y.S.V. Giving a Complete History of its Three Year Service in the War*. Greenwich, NY: People's Journal Book and Job Office, 1879.

Morris, W.S. *History Thirty-First Regiment Illinois Volunteer Infantry, Organized by John Logan*. Carbondale: Southern Illinois University Press, 1998.

Nichols, George Ward. *The Story of the Great March*. Williamstown, MA: Corner House Publishers, 1972.

Official Records (OR) of the War of the Rebellion, Series 1, Vol. 47, Part 1, Reports. Washington, D.C.: Government Printing Office, 1895.

Official Records (OR) of the War of the Rebellion, Series 1, Vol. 47, Part 2, Correspondence, etc. Washington, D.C.: Government Printing Office, 1895.

"Operations on the Atlantic Coast 1861–65 Virginia 1862, 1864 Vicksburg." Vol. 9, 1912. Military Historical Society of Massachusetts.

Osborne, Hartwell. *Trials and Triumphs: The Record of the Fifty-Fifth Ohio Volunteer Infantry*. Chicago: A.C. McClurge and Co., 1904.

Osborn, Thomas Ward. *The Fiery Trail: A Union Officer's Account of Sherman's Last Campaigns*. Knoxville: University of Tennessee Press, 1986.

Pepper, George W. *Personal Recollections of Sherman's Campaigns in Georgia and the Carolinas*. Zanefield, OH: Hugh Dunne, 1866.

Proceedings of the Massachusetts Historical Society. Vol. 49. Boston: The Society, 1916.

Recollections and Reminiscences, 1861–1865 through WWI. Vol. 1. Columbia: South Carolina Division of United Daughters of the Confederacy, 1998.

Recollections and Reminiscences, 1861–1865 through WWI. Vol. 4. Columbia: South Carolina Division of United Daughters of the Confederacy, 1998.

Rood, Hosea. *Story of the Service of Company E and the Twelfth Wisconsin Regiment, Veteran Volunteer Infantry, in the War of the Rebellion*, Milwaukee, WI: Swain and Tate Co. / Printers and Publishers, 1893.

Salley, Marion. *The Orangeburg Papers: The Writings of Marion Salley*. Vol. 1. Orangeburg, SC: Orangeburg County Historical and Genealogical Society, 1970.

SeCheverell, John H. *Journal History of the Twenty-Ninth Ohio*. Charleston, SC: Biliolife, 1883.

Sherman, W.T. *Memoirs of W.T. Sherman*. New York: Library of America, 1990.

Simms, William Gilmore. *Sack and Destruction of the City of Columbia, SC*. Atlanta: Power Press of Daily Phoenix, 1937.

Sligh, Charles R. *History of the Services of the First Regiment Michigan Engineers and Mechanics*. Grand Rapids, MI: 1921.

Stevenson, Thomas M. *History of the 78th O.V.V.I., From Its Muster In to Its Muster Out*. Zanesville, OH: Hugh Dunne, 1865.

Stoney, Samuel Gaillard. *The Dulles Family of South Carolina*. Columbia: University of South Carolina Press, 1955.

Swan, James B. *Chicago's Irish Legion: The 90th Illinois Volunteers in the Civil War*. Carbondale: Southern Illinois University Press, 2009

Trimble, Harvey M. *History of the Ninety-Third Regiment, Illinois Volunteer Infantry: From Organization to Muster Out*. Chicago: Blakely Printing Company, 1898.

Underwood, Adin Ballou. *The Three Year Service of the 33rd Massachusetts Infantry Regiment, 1862–1865*. Boston: A. Williams and Co., 1881.

Upson, Theodore. *With Sherman to the Sea, The Civil War Letters, Diaries, and Remembrances of Theodore F. Upson*. Baton Rouge: Louisiana State University Press, 1943.

Warner, Ezra. *Generals in Blue*. Baton Rouge: Louisiana State University Press, 1992.

———. *Generals in Gray*. Baton Rouge: Louisiana State University Press, 1995.

Wills, Charles Wright. *Army Life of an Illinois Soldier, Including a Day by Day Record of Sherman's March to the Sea*. Washington, D.C.: Globe Printing Company, 1906.

Wilson, Ephraim. *Memoirs of the War by Captain Ephraim Wilson of Co. G, 10th Illinois Veteran Volunteer Infantry.*. Cleveland, OH: W.M. Bayne Printing Company, 1893.

Wood, D.W. *History of the 20th Ohio Volunteer Infantry and Proceedings of the First Reunion*. Columbus, OH: Paul and Thrall Book and Job Printers, 1876.

ARTICLES

Moore, Sergeant John A. "A Glance at the Long Ago." *Bamberg Herald*, April 20, 1905.

Niles, H. "Governor Haynes' Inaugural Speech." *Niles Weekly Register* 43, no. 279 (1832).

Williams, Capt. Benjamin S. "A Confederate Soldier's Memoirs." *Charleston News*, March 8, 1914.

Index

About the Author

Growing up in the shadow of Sherman's battlegrounds near Orangeburg, South Carolina, Christopher Crabb is a graduate of Lipscomb University in Nashville, Tennessee. A gospel minister, Crabb and his wife, Julia, returned to South Carolina in 2008, now calling Colleton County home.

Visit us at
www.historypress.net